Chan Buddhism

Chan Buddhism

PETER D. HERSHOCK

Dimensions of Asian Spirituality

UNIVERSITY OF HAWAI'I PRESS

Honolulu

DIMENSIONS OF ASIAN SPIRITUALITY
Henry Rosemont, Jr., General Editor

This series makes available short but comprehensive works on specific Asian philosophical and religious schools of thought, works focused on a specific region, and works devoted to the full articulation of a concept central to one or more of Asia's spiritual traditions. Series volumes are written by distinguished scholars in the field who not only present their subject in historical context for the nonspecialist reader but also express their own views of the contemporary spiritual relevance of the subject for global citizens of the twenty-first century.

Library of Congress Cataloging-in-Publication Data
Hershock, Peter D.
Chan Buddhism / Peter D. Hershock.
p. cm. — (Dimensions of Asian spirituality ; v. 2)
Includes bibliographical references and index.
ISBN 0-8248-2780-5 (hardcover : alk. paper) —
ISBN 0-8248-2835-6 (pbk. : alk. paper)
1. Zen Buddhism—China—History. I. Title. II. Series.
BQ9262.9.C5H67 2004
294.3'927'0951—dc22
2004001348

University of Hawai'i Press books are printed on acid-free paper and meet the guidelines for permanence and durability of the Council on Library Resources.

Designed by Rich Hendel

Printed by The Maple-Vail Book Manufacturing Group

FRONTISPIECE: *Spirituality*, by Ni Peimin.
Reproduced with permission of the artist.

Contents

Editor's Preface

The University of Hawai'i Press has long been noted for its scholarly publications in and commitment to the field of Asian studies. This series, "Dimensions of Asian Spirituality," is in keeping with that commitment. It is a most appropriate time for such a series to appear. A number of the world's religions—major and minor—originated in Asia, continue to influence the lives of a third of the world's peoples, and should now be seen as global in scope, reach, and impact, with rich and varied resources for every citizen of the twenty-first century to explore.

Religion is at the heart of every culture. To be sure, the members of every culture have also been influenced by climate, geology, and the consequent patterns of economic activity they have developed for the production and distribution of goods. Only a rudimentary knowledge of physical geography is necessary to understand why African sculptors largely employed wood as their medium whereas their Italian Renaissance counterparts worked with marble. But while necessary for understanding cultures—not least our own—matters of geography and economics will not be sufficient: marble is found in China, too, yet the Chinese sculptor carved a bodhisattva, not a pietà, from his block.

In the same way, a mosque, synagogue, cathedral, stupa, and pagoda may be equally beautiful, but they are beautiful in different ways, and the differences cannot be accounted for merely on the basis of the materials used in their construction. Their beauty, their power to inspire awe and invite contemplation, rest largely on the religious view of the world—and the place of human beings in that world—expressed in their architecture. The spiritual dimensions of a culture are reflected significantly not only in art and architecture but in music, myths, poetry, rituals, customs, and patterns of social behavior as well. Therefore it follows that if we wish to understand why and how members of other cultures live as they do, we must understand the religious beliefs and practices to which they adhere.

In the first instance, such understanding of the "other" leads to tolerance, which is surely a good thing. Much of the pain and suffering in the world today is attributable to intolerance, a fear and hatred of those who look, think, and act differently. But as technological changes in communication, production, and transportation shrink the world, more and more people must confront the fact of human diversity in multiple forms—both between and within nations—and hence there is a growing need to advance beyond mere tolerance of difference to an appreciation and even celebration of it.

The evils attendant on intolerance notwithstanding, tolerance alone cannot contribute substantively to making the world a better—and sustainable—place for human beings to live. Mere tolerance is easy for us: I can fully respect your right to believe and worship as you wish, associate with whomever, and say what you will, simply by ignoring you. You assuredly have a right to speak, but not to make me listen.

Yet for most of us who live in economically developed societies, or are among the affluent in developing nations, tolerance is not enough. Ignoring the poverty, disease, and gross inequalities that afflict fully a third of the human race will only exacerbate, not alleviate, the conditions responsible for the misery that generates the violence becoming ever more commonplace throughout the world today. That violence will cease only when the more fortunate among the peoples of the world become active, take up the plight of the less fortunate, and resolve to create a more just world, a resolve that requires a full appreciation of everyone's co-humanity, significant differences in religious beliefs and practices notwithstanding.

Such appreciation should not, of course, oblige everyone to endorse all of the beliefs and practices within their own faith. A growing number of Catholics, for instance, support changes in church practice: a married clergy, the ordination of women, recognition of rights for gays and lesbians, and full reproductive rights for women. Yet they remain Catholics, believing that the tenets of their faith have the conceptual resources to bring about and justify these changes. In the same way, we can also believe—as a number of Muslim women do—that the Qur'an and other Islamic theological writings contain the conceptual resources to overcome the inferior status of women in some Muslim countries. And indeed we can believe that every spiritual tradition has within it the resources to counter older practices inimical to the full flourishing of all the faithful—including the faithful of other traditions as well.

Another reason to advance beyond mere tolerance to appreciation and celebration of the many and varied forms of spiritual expression is virtually a truism: the more we look through the window of another culture's beliefs and practices, the more it becomes a mirror of our own (even for those who follow no religious tradition). We must look carefully and charitably, however, or the reflections become distorted. When studying other religions, most people are inclined to focus on cosmological and ontological questions: What do these people believe about the origin of the world and where it is heading? Do they believe in ghosts? Immortal souls? A creator god?

Answering such metaphysical questions is of course necessary for understanding and appreciating the specific forms and content of the art, music, architecture, rituals, and traditions inspired by the specific religion under study. But the sensitive—and sensible—student will bracket the further question of whether the metaphysical pronouncements are literally true—we must attend carefully to the metaphysics (and theologies) of the religions we study, but questions of their literal truth should be set aside in order to concentrate on a different question: How could a thoughtful, thoroughly decent human being subscribe to such beliefs and attendant practices?

Studied in this light, we may come to appreciate how each religious tradition provides a coherent account of a world not fully amenable to human manipulation or, perhaps, even to full human understanding. The metaphysical pronouncements of the world's religions of course differ measurably from faith to faith, and each has had a significant influence on the physical expressions of the respective faith in synagogues, stupas, mosques, pagodas, and cathedrals. Despite these differences between the buildings, however, the careful and sensitive observer can see the spiritual dimensions of human life that these sacred structures share and express. In the same way we can come to appreciate the common spiritual dimensions of each religion's differing metaphysics and theology: While the several traditions give different answers to the question of the meaning *of* life, they provide a multiplicity of guidelines and spiritual disciplines to enable everyone to find meaning *in* life: in this world. By plumbing the spiritual depths of other religious traditions, then, we may come to explore more deeply the spiritual resources of our own, and at the same time diminish the otherness of the other and create a more peaceable and just world in which everyone can find meaning in their all-too-human lives.

ABOUT THIS VOLUME

Buddhism is one of the oldest of the world's spiritual traditions, transforming—and being transformed by—virtually all of the cultures of South, Southeast, and East Asia, and is today global in scope; it remains the major religion in Thailand, Tibet, Laos, Myanmar, Cambodia, Sri Lanka, and Japan, and at least some Buddhists can be found in almost every nation-state throughout the region.

Having to adapt to cultural differences as they spread from its original home in India and developing an increasing set of conceptually rich canonical texts, Buddhist traditions multiplied over the centuries. In the West, especially the United States, the Chan tradition, better known by its Japanese name, Zen, has become paradigmatic of Buddhist spirituality. The Japanese have made many original contributions to the development of this tradition, which has exercised considerable influence on many dimensions of Japanese culture. But Chan Buddhism began in China and developed there for several centuries before migrating eastward, and knowledge of that beginning and development is prerequisite for a fuller understanding of what Chan Buddhism is and is not.

In this volume Peter Hershock presents an admirably clear and succinct account of the genesis of Buddhism in India and the Chinese historical and philosophical context in which Chan emerged as a unique expression of Buddhist spirituality. He is eminently qualified for the task, being solidly grounded in both sinology and philosophy. Equally important, Hershock is a practicing Buddhist, so the reader can be assured that what follows is not merely a factual account of people, places, events, and ideas. All of these particulars have their proper place in his narrative, but Hershock's focus is on Chan as a living, vibrant tradition of great relevance today for everyone, not Asians alone.

Chan is commonly understood as iconoclastic, and in a number of respects it surely was—and is. But many of the stereotypical beliefs about Zen are just that: stereotypes; hence Hershock himself is often the iconoclast in these pages, correcting a number of common misperceptions of what Chan is about.

One such misunderstanding concerns the extent of Chan iconoclasm itself. Many readers may well be surprised by the wealth of rituals, customs, and traditions Hershock describes as central to Chan.

A second misunderstanding centers on the concept of enlightenment in Chan, usually described as sudden, as the be-all and end-all of Buddhist religious experience, once attained, altogether enduring. Not so, argues our author: an important event in one's life perhaps—if it occurs—but the ultimate goal is less to *see* the world aright than to *live* in the world aright; Chan practices are a lifelong endeavor.

Still a third common misunderstanding about the Chan tradition is that it is ruggedly individualistic. While this picture may be appealing to some in competitive capitalist societies, the picture has been greatly overdrawn, according to Hershock. To be sure, the four Chan masters whose biographies he narrates—and many other masters as well—seem not so much to march as to leap and bound through the pages of Buddhist history; unique individuals they surely were, and Hershock celebrates them as such. But he equally stresses the communal nature of Chan practices, both with regard to the collectivity of monks in a monastery and also as a goal of Chan practice, that allow us to realize "liberating intimacy" (the title of Hershock's first book on Chan), to get rid of the habits and ego boundaries that prevent us from being fully open to and with our fellow human beings.

In sum, while there is an important truth in the Chan saying "Every flower is the prettiest," the same cannot be said for introductory books on the Chan tradition itself; some are much better than others, and this is one of them. Read on.

HENRY ROSEMONT, JR.

Acknowledgments

I would first like to thank Henry Rosemont, Jr., for inviting me to be a part of this series of books on Asian spiritualities in practice and for being such a careful and caring series editor. As so pointedly demonstrated by the first years of this new millennium, the need for cross-cultural understanding—especially understanding across religious boundaries—has never been more important and imperative. I am honored to have been given the chance to contribute to a series that will bring the sense and sensibility of Asia's spiritual traditions to the wider public beyond the scholarly world of the academy.

I would also like to thank the many scholars from whose work I have learned much regarding the history and texts of Chan Buddhism. Without their dedication to the scholarly craft, this book would have not have been possible. Among them, Ronald Epstein, who served as an outside reader for the series, deserves special mention for his helpful comments during preparation of the final version of the book.

Finally, I would like to thank my Buddhist teachers. Seung Sahn Dae Soen Sa Nim first introduced me to the practice and stories of the Korean branch of Chan. He is also responsible for having sent me to Ji Kwang Dae Poep Sa Nim, under whose guidance, remonstrance, and limitless compassion I have practiced Buddhism for nearly two decades. The trust that she has placed in me, her continuous encouragement to develop the virtues of a teacher, and—above all—her own teachings have been the foundation on which my understanding of Chan has been built. I cannot thank her enough.

Introduction

This is not a book about enlightenment. It is a book about enlightening practice. More specifically, it is a philosophical introduction to the practice tradition of Chan Buddhism—the Chinese forebear of Korean Son and Japanese Zen.

Many people become interested in Buddhism because they believe it promises a way of transcending the trials of everyday life. According to this belief, practicing Buddhism eventually results in the consummate experience of release or freedom from suffering—the personal attainment of enlightenment. Often, this is imagined as a brilliant opening through which the practitioner passes once and for all into the extraordinary—a gateway to infinite spiritual bliss and completion.

Chan Buddhism does not promise any such extraordinary state of full and final spiritual attainment. Indeed, it explicitly insists that there is ultimately nothing to attain. The path of enlightening all beings, Chan master Mazu notes, is just "ordinary mind." Of course, it is ordinary mind with a difference: the absence of any boundary or horizon on the other side of which lies something "more" or "better" or "mystically complete."

Chan Buddhists do use metaphors of doors or gateways in explaining how one enters the spirit of Chan. But they refer to passages that open fully into the world, not out of it. Passing through the gate of Chan is to leave behind the narrowness of the self and its binding destinies. Chan directs us into an unending process of cultivating and demonstrating both appreciative and contributory virtuosity—a horizonless capacity for according with our situation and responding as needed. This is not freedom from the world and its relationships but tirelessly within them.

The genealogy of Chan is traditionally traced back to the Buddha and his mind-to-mind transmission of the Dharma to Mahakasyapa in the fifth century B.C.E. By the time Chan teachings began circulating in the late sixth or early seventh century C.E., Buddhism had been spreading and diversifying in alternating waves of cultural accommodation and countercultural advocacy for over a thousand years throughout India, Central Asia, Tibet, Southeast Asia, and East Asia. Forged in China by dramatic virtuosos responding to intense and chronic personal, communal, and cultural crisis, Chan was arguably the most iconoclastic, sober, and yet brilliantly celebratory branch of the Buddhist family tree. Today—especially in the West—it remains the ancestral source of some of the most vibrant forms of Buddhist thought and practice.

With surprising earthiness, discourse records from the first centuries of Chan reveal a spirited and diverse community in which the voice of authority is in turns audacious and egalitarian, profoundly deferential and irreverent, fiercely humorous and heroically uninhibited. In the practice tradition of Chan, the hallmark of excellence is not the ability to transmit a fixed canon or act according to set customs and principles. It is unprecedented and yet skilled immediacy or improvisational genius.

In a thirteenth-century compilation of anecdotes and commentaries, the *Gateless Frontier Pass (Wumen guan)*, the dramatic tone of Chan is expressed in a striking, exclamatory vignette: "On the cliff-edge of life and death, commanding complete freedom! Among the six paths of embodiment and the four forms of birth, reveling in joyous and playful attentive virtuosity *(samadhi)!*"* With utterly refreshing candor, Chan calls on us to celebrate the enlightening possibilities given right here and now. It offers no substantial rewards and no specific experiential treasures: only the means of realizing unwavering confidence for entering into ever deeper and more liberating intimacy with our immediate surroundings. In this sense, Chan awakening is no private affair, but an irreducibly social process. Whether we are standing, sitting, walking, or lying down, Chan means realizing horizonless and responsive presence with and for one another.

Like a fiery jazz performance, Chan's responsive immediacy alone might command one's attention. As is true of virtuoso musical performances, the words and actions through which the spirit of Chan

---

* All translations included are my own. Readers interested in full translations of quoted texts should refer to the narrative bibliography (Further Reading). References are provided for both Chinese editions of relevant texts and full English translations.

is demonstrated are uplifting reminders of human potentials. Even momentary encounters with them have clear benefits, vastly extending the horizons of what we might have believed humanly possible. But attention to such peak performances is, for most of us, quite fleeting. Even the most profound performances are quickly turned into fading memories, and the vast potentials to which they had directed us remain precisely that.

It would be a shame if such passing exposure were to exhaust our encounter with Chan. A quarter of a century ago, the Tibetan Buddhist teacher Chogyam Trungpa called attention to the temptations of "spiritual materialism." By this, he was referring to the consumption of wisdom tradition "commodities" from around the world in a ravenous search for something more or different or better. Chan consolidated at an analogous point in China's history, when an entire population was desperately hungry for effective, spiritual sustenance. In an overall environment alternately verging on collapse and on history-making leaps forward, Chan arose out of a need to respond immediately, surely, and helpfully to situations for which history cannot have prepared us and in which absolute principles are manifestly inappropriate. Practicing Chan is about successfully, gracefully, and even gratefully navigating uncharted and unpredictable seas.

Chan thus has a relevance that is invariably timely—and perhaps especially so for those of us who are living in times of unparalleled social, political, economic, and cultural change. Daily, we are reminded that ours is not a world built on long-established foundations. On the contrary, it is a world being built on the run, a world in which change is not just given, but rapidly accelerating. Long relied-upon practices and values are being fundamentally questioned—and often abandoned and replaced—at dizzying rates. And still we seem to be stumbling headlong from crisis to crisis with no end in sight. Chan opens breaks in the pattern: a way of liberating all beings with tireless virtuosity, resolving the trouble in any situation whatsoever, especially when there is nothing at all that we can rely on.

A crucial part of Chan's response to the spiritual malaise of medieval China was its radical dismissal of the need for intermediaries—whether Indian texts, local religious adepts, or supramundane bodhisattvas. Thus, Chan master Huineng insisted that "it is precisely practicing Buddhism that is the Buddha." His point was not lost on his audience: if "our own minds are the place of enlightenment," then China must be able to produce homegrown buddhas of its own. The ninth patriarch, Linji, took this notion to its iconoclastic extreme, telling his students to stop seeking either "enlightenment" or "the Buddha" altogether. Indeed he proclaimed, "Should you see the Buddha on the road, kill him!" In the end, we can only rely on ourselves to reshape the relationships that are sponsoring the suffering all around us. The responsibility for bringing about an enlightening situation is finally *our* own.

The Chan tradition thus arose as a response to the growing need of Chinese to take Buddhism truly to heart—and not just ordained clergy but laypeople as well. Unlike prior traditions of Chinese Buddhism, Chan was distinctive in taking the teachings of Chinese-born masters as basic "texts." They did not make use of the highly sophisticated vocabularies that were present in the Indian Buddhist texts and commentaries, and in their Chinese translations and emulations. Chan literature was written in the vocabulary of everyday speech. This vernacular style of writing was ideally suited to tailoring Buddhist teachings and practices to the concrete needs of Chinese society and speaking to the spiritual longings of people turned skeptical about the ability of Confucian and Daoist rituals and teachings to meet the challenges of the times.

Like medieval China, the contemporary Western world exhibits great economic and political promise but is also deeply troubled and spiritually enervated. Alternatives to our inherited systems of values are being urgently sought in virtually every part of society. There is widespread conviction that our own history cannot prepare us for tomorrow but also an equally widespread conviction that our troubles are, finally, our own to resolve. Far from diminishing, with our collective rush into postmodernity and the increasing speed of our technological juggernaut, the relevance of Chan Buddhism is, if anything, growing.

This book is a very modest attempt to express a space within which the contemporary relevance of Chan might be more fully appreciated, by non-Buddhists and Buddhists alike. Studying Chan Buddhism recommends itself not only for intrinsic reasons but also because it can help us to better situate ourselves in our own histories. The story of Chan is one of cultural assimilations, border crossings, crises of faith, and realizing a muscular readiness to evidence compassionate moral clarity. It is also a story about finding—in our own day-to-day relationships—the resources needed to challenge successfully the way things are and to turn our situation in a resolutely enlightening direction.

The story of Chan Buddhism cannot be understood, however, without having a basic working knowledge of its Buddhist heritage and the Chinese cultural environment into which Buddhist concepts and practices were eventually imported. My narrative approach to Chan will thus begin by briefly rehearsing the origins of Buddhism in Vedic India as a spiritual counterculture that offered systematic strategies for resolving human suffering. After introducing the central teachings and practices held in common throughout the Buddhist world, I will sketch the broad historical pattern of Buddhism's diversification in response to changing circumstances and provide a brief summary of Buddhism's first centuries in China.

The unique contribution made by Buddhism to China's spiritual life can only be appreciated by understanding the ways in which Buddhism both resonated with and differed from the indigenous Chinese traditions of Confucianism and Daoism. These traditions will be introduced with an eye toward highlighting the process of cultural accommodation and advocacy by means of which Buddhism took root in Chinese soil and eventually became a truly Chinese spiritual tradition. Here, the roles played by translation and meditation will serve as an organizing theme, with particular emphasis on how Buddhism adapted to the needs of its new Chinese audience and the role played in this response by the teachings of karma, interdependence, and buddha-nature.

The best contemporary scholarship has effectively challenged the internal myths of Chan's origins, making it clear that Chan was not born all at once, in one place, at one time. Instead, it suggests that the traditional genealogy and identity of Chan was quilted together over a period of some hundred and fifty years. As interesting and important as this scholarly narrative is, however, it is the dramatically unified emergence of Chan as depicted in its own narrative traditions that best captures the force of Chan's unique approach to Buddhist practice and spirituality as understood from within. And it is to these traditional narratives that I will turn in following the arc of Chan's birth and maturation, examining in some detail a particular genealogical thread in the traditional narrative "quilt" of Chan practice: the lineage that runs from Bodhidharma through Huineng, Mazu, and Linji. These four masters continue to be central to the Chan imagination, most powerfully and effectively exemplifying the unique character of Chan spirituality.

To create a usefully general bridge to our own contemporary experience, I will follow this reading of Chan in its own terms with a philosophical "reconstruction" of Chan practice. Here the aim is to provide a coherent framework, in relatively nontechnical terms, for understanding the system of Chan practice. Particular emphasis will be placed on the ultimately performative and relational nature of Chan awakening and its contemporary relevance.

A final word is appropriate here about including a book on Buddhism —and, in particular, Chan Buddhism—in a series on Asian spiritualities. As the notion has most commonly been used in the Western world, spirituality directs us toward what is above and beyond nature and the immediate circumstances of our embodiment. On the face of it, this does not seem like a Buddhist sensibility. If all things are seen as interdependent—a basic Buddhist teaching—then there cannot be ultimate dividing lines between mind and body or between spirit and nature.

But if attending to what lies above and beyond nature and our immediate situation is not understood as crossing a metaphysical boundary into the supernatural, but rather as a matter of dissolving our habits of exclusion and relinquishing our customary horizons for what we allow to be relevant—a process of restoring our original intimacy with all things—Buddhism can be seen as a profoundly spiritual tradition. It is a spirituality devoted to erasing the fearful anguish of feeling utterly alone in this world and to resuming full presence as an appreciative and contributing part of it. It is with such an understanding that this introduction to Chan Buddhism has been written.

CHAPTER 1

The Buddhist Roots of Chan

Buddhism originated in northern India some 2,500 years ago as a response to the suffering inherent in the human condition. Beginning in his own lifetime, the teachings of Siddhartha Gautama—the Buddha, or "Awakened One"—were quickly spread throughout India, and, over a period of five or six centuries, they were carried across the entire continent of Asia. With the rise of transoceanic commerce and politics from the seventeenth century onward, Buddhist teachings and practices spread into Africa, Europe, and the Americas and now exercise a truly global reach.

Unlike the other major world religions, Buddhism is not organized around a universally shared core text like the Vedas, the Bible, or the Qur'an. There is no central source of Buddhist authority. Neither are there any globally fixed institutions or ritual frameworks. Translated into English, the collected teachings of the Buddha would fill several dozen thousand-page books. While the Dalai Lama is globally revered as an exemplary Buddhist, he is actually only the preeminent leader of a single Tibetan school of Buddhism. For many Western Buddhists, although it is important to respect the diverse Asian heritages of Buddhist thought and practice, it is equally or more important to subject them to critical review and revision. Indeed, it is tempting to say that there is no "Buddhism" but only many "Buddhisms."

While a careful and comprehensive introduction to the entire Buddhist "family tree" is neither possible nor appropriate here, Chan Buddhism cannot be understood without at least broadly locating it in the genealogy of Buddhist traditions as well as in the development of Chinese culture. Family trees are often represented as self-contained patterns. But, in fact, every branch marks a point of intimate contact and mutual contribution between previously distinct histories—that is, between the meaningful and complex life stories of both persons and peoples. In the case of Buddhism and especially the Chinese development of Chan, this interweaving and eventual interpenetration of histories has been particularly complex and deep.

The Indian Birth of Buddhist Thought and Practice

In the sixth century B.C.E., the subcontinent of India was in the midst of a cultural and intellectual tidal shift. Between eight hundred and a thousand years earlier, nomadic Aryan peoples from Central Asia had crossed the Khyber Pass to settle on the Ganges plain. For reasons that remain unclear, the powerful urban centers that had characterized the indigenous Harappan culture from the middle of the third millennium B.C.E. had for the most part already been abandoned. Aided by the advent of iron tools and weaponry, large agricultural communities were gradually consolidated under Aryan rule, and there developed the distinctive social, political, economic, and religious institutions that would dominate the life of the subcontinent for centuries thereafter. By the sixth century, however, the pressures resulting from expanding political states, increasing urban development, and the rise of a monetary economy were opening deep fissures in the authority of the dominant aristocratic and religious elites. In particular, criticism began circulating of the beliefs and ritual practices derived from the collection of Indo-Aryan religious hymns known as the Vedas as well as of the social structures these implied.

For nearly a thousand years, memorizing the Vedas and implementing the rituals derived from them had been the sole province of hereditary priests, or brahmins. In accordance with beliefs embedded in the Vedas, brahmins and aristocratic rulers and warriors occupied the upper reaches of society. At a great social distance below were members of the caste responsible for such work as farming, herding, commerce, and construction. At the very bottom were members of the caste who did work like making leather or butchering animals that were taken to be inherently impure. There was no social mobility between these castes. And although all people could be said to have four aims in life—*artha* (material goods and comfort), *kama* (sensual or aesthetic enrichment), dharma (the proper exercise of duty to family, society, and the gods), and *moksha* (liberation)—only brahmins could reasonably hope to attain all four. All members of society could (and, indeed, were fully expected to) do their duty and enjoy proper levels and degrees of material goods and sensuous pleasures. But only properly observant brahmins could hope to realize complete freedom from the limitations of having an individual existence, merging with the limitless and eternal cosmic principle known as Brahman. For others, that would have to wait for another (brahmin) lifetime.

With the erosion of the authority of the Vedic elite came a concerted questioning of the meaning and restricted possibilities of liberation. A new class of religious practitioners—*sramana*s, or "strivers" —emerged from the non-brahmin castes. They held that the truth of human life could be accessed by anyone, regardless of caste, through the exercise of reason and meditative discipline. The contemplative and ascetic practices undertaken by these strivers toward spiritual freedom may in part represent a resurgence of indigenous traditions from pre-Aryan India. There is no doubt, however, that they forever changed the face of Indian religion.

Over a relatively short time, a very wide spectrum of beliefs came to enjoy currency in India. At one end lay the orthodox traditions based on brahminical interpretations of the Vedic hymns and their philosophical extension in the body of literature known as the Upanishads. Considerable variation in practical and philosophical emphases were evident among these orthodox expressions of Vedic religiosity. But all aimed to make the best possible sense out of a general worldview according to which each individual being exists only provisionally and in which ultimate reality is a singular consciousness-existence-bliss most commonly referred to as Brahman. The apparent separation of individual beings—both from one another and from the universal godhead or divine awareness—was taken, in one fashion or another, to be a function of illusion, or *maya,* and the effect of morally weighted action, or karma. Only through release from illusion and the chain of cause and effect binding us to the round of births and deaths could our true selves (atman) be restored into union *(yoga)* with the infinite absoluteness of Brahman.

At the other end of the spectrum lay rational materialists who denied the existence of souls or true selves, the operation of moral— as opposed to natural—laws, and the ultimate reality of a limitless and thus immaterial godhead or divine force. Instead, they insisted that nothing survives the death of the body, that good and evil are human constructs, and that reality is essentially and thoroughly material. Like many present-day scientists, such proponents of materialism generally argued that real liberation was not some imagined release from the world, but the power of making and acting on choices in it. The most extreme of these advocated indulging sense desires without restraint or restriction in a hedonistic celebration of individual freedom, with no thought of future lives and consequences that would in fact never come.

Arrayed between these extremes were various traditions more concerned with finding the correct practice for realizing *moksha* rather than absolute doctrines about "reality." Most often, these groups advocated the immediate rejection of family life, material comforts, familial and communal duties, caste identification, and the concerted practice of one or another form of ascetic self-discipline and/or contemplation. Through a process of literal abstraction, many such traditions aimed to cut the practitioner free of all but the most tenuous threads of connection with worldly life and experience—freedom from virtually any cause of perceived bondage. Other traditions, like those that found fullest expression in the epic philosophical drama of the *Bhagavad-Gita,* were more explicitly conservative and advocated union or *yoga* simply through doing one's own duty, without regard to consequences and the appearance of right and wrong.

It was into a world of such complexly competing views of liberation that Siddhartha Gautama was born into the royal family of a small kingdom in the foothills of the Himalayas. By the time he was of an age to marry, the young prince had already seen that, even for the most privileged people, suffering was a constant possibility and eventual reality. According to the most widely accepted narratives, it was not long after marrying and fathering a son that he decided to renounce his right to the throne and become a *sramana,* or seeker of truth. For six years, he practiced under a variety of masters of contemplative and ascetic practice. A dedicated and brilliantly adept student, he demonstrated a rare capacity for realizing the essence of each master's practices, and all invited him to carry on their work. None, however, was able to provide Siddhartha with the answer he was seeking—insight into the meaning and resolution of all suffering, for all beings. Despite all his achievements in terms of altered states of consciousness and mystical insight, that eluded him.

Finally, he abandoned his ascetic regimen and his anxious seeking after truth. Stationing himself under a tree in a secluded area, he sat down calmly determined to realize the truth of things and to cut completely through the mystery of suffering, opening a path to its full resolution. One breath at a time, he settled into unhindered and horizonless presence. In the final hour before dawn, he succeeded, becoming a "buddha," or "enlightened one," freeing himself forever from the "wound of existence" and the compelling and compulsive round of birth and death.

In communicating the meaning of his awakening to others, he often referred to it as the reopening of a long-neglected Middle Way. At one level, his awakening cleared a viable path between those claiming the complete annihilation of the person at death and those claiming the eternal existence of an essential self, between those calling for unwavering hedonism and those calling for equally relentless asceticism. But more generally it was a healing restoration of the normally excluded middle ground between "is" and "is-not," between cause and effect, mind and matter, self and other, and independence and dependence.

In effect, the Buddha taught a way of refraining from taking a stand on any of the positions from which his contemporaries viewed the human condition and its cosmic context. His Middle Path was not a matter of assuming some midway point between the extremes at either end of the spectrum of beliefs prevalent in India but an alternative to the entire spectrum itself. As such, his teachings were—indeed, could not avoid being—deeply countercultural.

Among the most apparent practical expressions of his Middle Path was his founding of an extended community of seekers known as the sangha. Unlike his contemporaries, the Buddha did not advocate a total and complete break from community as a means of realizing liberation. Rather, he acknowledged the benefits of total commitment to practicing meditation, free from the daily concerns of the householder's life. But at the same time, he extolled the importance of the "good friend" in following the Middle Path and urged his students to live together in an alternative, monastic community organized to promote intensified practice. For those who chose to remain householders—taking, in some ways, the steeper approach to the Middle Way—he provided guidelines for revising the meaning of their social relationships in ways conducive to the realization of full liberation from suffering. This emphasis on mutual support and the relevance of relationships to realization of enlightenment would later be central to the conception and development of Chan.

Importantly, among the Buddha's students who realized full awakening, there were both laypeople and ordained members of the sangha, drawn from all castes and both male and female. The acceptance of women as candidates for the practice of spiritual discipline marked a particularly radical departure from the norms of the day. By freely admitting women and the members of the lowest castes into his community, he not only denied the significance of elite status, he denied the significance of any essential status whatsoever. What truly mattered were not one's "state of affairs" or "identity," but the direction and quality of one's attention and conduct.

Perhaps no less radical was the Buddha's insistence that his own speech patterns and language not be considered crucial elements in the spread of his teachings, or Dharma. Urging his students to use local patterns of speech and local dialects in spreading the Dharma, the Buddha made it clear that great learning and intellectual sophistication were not necessary for liberation. One did not need the ability to read sacred texts, the talent for reciting and understanding convoluted doctrines, or the means and institutional authority to perform complex rituals. Neither did one need to be able to enter into winning debate with the advocates of the hundreds of views on "ultimate truth" that were then current in India. One needed only to keenly attend to how things have come to be, just as they are. This alone was needed to see the way of fully and meaningfully resolving suffering.

The Buddha's Root Teachings

According to the Buddha, the first step in liberation—the first step on the Middle Path of Buddhist practice—is to come fully to rest and realize that *something is wrong here.*

It may be that you are in the midst of the breakup of a love relationship. A family member or friend might recently have passed away. Or it may be that you are worried about an upcoming interview or exam, dizzy with hunger after missing your last meal, or simply worn out to the verge of exhaustion by the demands of parenthood. Whether it is a matter of dreams evaporating before our eyes, efforts going unrewarded, or a shock wave of terrorism breaking altogether too close to home, right now, things are going awry.

Hearing this, there is a compulsion to object. Having just eaten, you feel full and content. Having just received a long sought after raise or succeeded in catching the eye of an attractive classmate or coworker, "something is wrong here" doesn't ring quite true. There is no doubt that love relationships often fail and dissolve into spells of deep depression and sharp self-doubt. But what could be more right than the feeling of falling in love? What could be more joyous than the birth of a first child or the moment of a dream come finally true? What was the Buddha's point?

THE FOUR NOBLE TRUTHS

As he traveled from village to village and from town to town, the Buddha was often asked what he taught and how it differed from the teachings of other homeless ascetics and contemplatives as well as from those given by local brahmin interpreters of the Vedas and Upanishads. Most often, he would reply that his Dharma, or teaching, was very simple, consisting of only four simple truths that he would invite his audience to consider:

1. All this is *duhkha* ("troubled" or "suffering").
2. There is a pattern in how *duhkha* arises.
3. There is a pattern in how *duhkha* is resolved.
4. There is an Eightfold Path for turning *duhkha* toward meaningful resolution.

Like many of the first translators to render Buddhist texts into Western languages, many of those who heard these Four Noble Truths would dismiss the first truth as a statement of unlimited and finally useless pessimism: "everything is suffering." But the first noble truth actually makes no such universal claim. The Buddha said, "All *this* is troubled or suffering." He would agree that we can eat a chicken salad or a hamburger and get rid of our hunger pains—at least for several hours. But aside from the fact that this "solution" is not a lasting one, there is the problem of perspective. Is eating a hamburger a trouble-free solution to the problem of hunger in our present situation as a whole?

For example, how must this "solution" appear to chickens and cows? How are Central American peasants affected by the beef industry's forced conversion of subsistence farmland to grazing—a crucial link in servicing fast food cravings? The first noble truth invites us to resist acting as if such differences in perspective do not really matter. They do. The fact that "I'm okay" does not necessarily entail that "you're okay." Realizing that all *this*—our situation as a whole—is troubled or suffering involves opening ourselves up to seeing that, right now, from some present perspective, things are not going well.

The second noble truth suggests that if we look closely enough, we discover that there is a pattern in things going wrong and that we are invariably at least part of the reason why. We are led by our usual perspective on the suffering and trouble all about us to see their origins as lying well outside of us. Suffering and trouble are caused by others, or by fate, or by just plain bad luck. The second noble truth insists on our seeing things otherwise.

Unlike pain, *duhkha* does not arise because of any single cause but through a network of situation-specific, interdependent conditions. Consider two children racing across a playground. The boy is a step behind the girl and reaches out to catch hold of her shirt. She loses her balance and goes down in a rolling tangle. Sitting up, her knees and elbows scraped and bleeding, she cries. One can explain the pain she feels in strictly linear, causal terms. Her limbs hit the ground at a velocity great enough that the impact tears the skin. Nerve endings in the area send signals to the brain announcing this violation of bodily integrity. This is experienced as pain. With some antibiotic gel, a few bandages, and a warm hug, the pain can be eased enough for her to smile and go on playing.

But what if the boy is her best friend? As she stares at the blood welling up out of her scraped knees, the girl suffers from much more than bodily damage. She is wondering how he could have cheated just to win a playground race. Best friends are not supposed to do that. Days, months, even years later, she will be affected by this betrayal of basic trust. The relationship, perhaps, will never be the same.

In this example, the girl's suffering arises not only through the impact of her limbs on hard ground. It arises depending, as well, on certain values regarding friendship and what it can and cannot include. It depends on her personal history and how she interprets her friend's act of catching hold of her shirt and causing her to fall. Perhaps he was only trying to slow her down, not pull her down. Or perhaps he was trying to make a point to her: "You have been making the highest test scores in math because you cheat, and cheating always hurts someone." Suffering arises, in other words, through a complex set of conditions that include easily observed "facts" but also broadly shared cultural values, personal histories, and individual beliefs about what things can and cannot mean.

Suffering is thus not as easy to treat as simple pain. Dealing with suffering requires understanding exactly what kind of cultural and personal impasse has been reached, what "normal" expectations have been violated, and which parts of the situation are taken to be negotiable and which are not. When a child dies in early infancy, the tragedy "naturally" seems much greater than when a grandparent dies. This is not because there is any objective difference in the process of dying or because there is any good time for death to occur. The difference is, at bottom, cultural. When an older person passes away we may find it easier to accept because we believe they have lived a full life. The death of an infant seems premature—a violation of the way things should be. But we could just as well think that the death of an older person leaves behind many more severed relationships, a much greater emotional vacuum than does the death of an infant. In cultures where being human is considered an achievement, and persons are understood as irreducibly relational in nature, a miscarriage may not warrant either soul-searching or suffering. For a woman who conceived a child in a short-lived, extramarital affair, a miscarriage may even be experienced with a sad measure of relief.

From this, Buddhism does not conclude that suffering is not truly real. It is real. But like all things, suffering arises conditionally—as part of a pattern of interdependence in which we (and our perspectives) always play a part. In explaining the second noble truth, the Buddha often made use of a heuristic or learning device called the twelvefold chain of interdependent origination. The origin of suffering, he said, can be seen as a wheel-like constellation of interconnected conditions including ignorance, habit formations, consciousness, name and form, the six sense organs, sensory contacts, feelings, cravings, and attachments. That is, suffering cannot be dissociated from patterns in what we ignore, from patterns in how we interact, and from our sense of self-identity. At the core of all our troubled and troubling situations are our beliefs about who we are and who we are not. Underlying these are more or less conscious senses of what should and should not happen, our particular wants or desires, and the limits these project for what we are responsible for and what we are not.

In summarizing all this, the Buddha often remarked that the root of all our suffering is the conceit that "I am"—the arrogance of thinking that we are essentially independent beings and not intimately connected with and a part of all things. "Is and is-not," he said, "are the twin barbs on which all humankind is impaled." The arrogance of independence and the degradation of dependence are two sides of the same coin. There is never one without the other. Insisting on our independent existence or on essential differences between "humanity" and "nature," or between "mind" and "body" or "self" and "other" is to ignore the immeasurably rich middle ground between them. As with any form of ignorance, this cannot lead to any ultimate security but only to increasingly deep vulnerability.

If the second noble truth alerts us to our implication in the arising of *duhkha,* the third truth asks us to see that we are always in a position to be part of its resolution. In brief, this means restoring the horizonless middle ground of our interdependence with all things. Healing the wound of existence—our presumed, essential separateness from all things—is something only we can do. The method of doing so is outlined in the Noble Eightfold Path, the fourth truth of practically developing right view, right intention, right speech, right action, right livelihood, right effort, right mindfulness, and right meditation.

Traditionally, the Eightfold Path was understood as a comprehensive, three-dimensional response to troubled or troubling situations

—the systematic practice of wisdom, attentive virtuosity, and moral clarity. Instead of being a once-and-for-all solution, the Eightfold Path opens up a way of continuously reorienting our lives away from samsara (in a Buddhist sense; chronic and intense suffering and trouble) toward nirvana (the liberating resolution of all suffering or trouble).

The Four Noble Truths are not a teaching that tells us how things really are. They are not doctrines about the nature of "absolute reality" or an attempt to explain the specific causes of our present state of affairs. Instead, these truths offer a strategy for changing the meaning of our situation or where we are heading. Failing to understand this reduces any encounter with Buddhism to a matter of reading recipes without ever cooking and eating a meal. Buddhist teachings are directions for revising or transforming our relationships. They can be deeply nourishing but only if we "cook" with them in the midst of our own circumstances.

THE TEACHING OF THE THREE MARKS

Nowhere did the Buddha press this point more forcefully than in teaching the three "marks" of impermanence, absence of self, and *duhkha*. Ironically, this teaching has been particularly prone to being interpreted as a doctrine about how things really are. In fact, it enjoins us to practice seeing all things as impermanent, as absent of any abiding essence or identity, and as troubled or troubling. The difference between "are" and "as" is highly significant.

Duhkha

Because I have already raised the problem of *duhkha* in discussing the first noble truth, let me begin with the final "mark." For most people, seeing all things as troubled or troubling is the last thing they want to do. Why would we want to go around being so utterly pessimistic, constantly "ruining" our situation by always picking out what is wrong with it?

First, recall that realizing the first noble truth means seeing moment by moment that happiness always comes at some cost to someone or something. Far from being an exercise in hopeless pessimism, seeing all things as troubled or troubling means finding a way to understand one's own situation from another's perspective. In effect, this means opening up connections that allow us to realize a shared presence. Doing so is the basis of entering into ever-deepening community.

Fundamentally, this means becoming aware that, in some way, we all make a difference to one another. We thus begin seeing that we have a responsibility for asking what kind of difference. In this way, seeing all things as troubled or troubling establishes the foundation or roots for cultivating the felt partnership of true compassion. Through it, we not only begin healing the "wound of existence," we begin dissolving the conceit that "I am" and the habitual violence of excluding from concern all that "I am not."

Impermanence

The invitation to see all things as impermanent meets with a related form of resistance. As a doctrine about how things are, it would seem to be an invitation to falsehood. Although it is not always easy to observe, all material objects change—even the sun and the stars. Far easier to observe are the changes in our own minds and feelings, and in our relationships with others. But can the same be said of all things? What about mathematical truths or natural laws? What about the universe as a whole? Pressed to answer similar questions—for example, "is the world eternal or not eternal?"—the Buddha customarily remained silent. At other times, he would refuse to take a stand on either "this" or "that"—that is, on either side of the opposition posed by the question.

Practically, we can see all things as impermanent regardless of whether or not natural laws or mathematical truths are maintained to be unchanging. To what end, though, would we do so? To begin with, it becomes impossible to assume—or even hope—that one can hold onto anything forever. This very decisively undercuts the kinds of expectation that lead to so much of our disappointment and suffering. But at the same time, it makes it impossible for us to hold onto the assumption that there is nothing we can do to change our circumstances. Seeing all things as continuously changing is to see that no situation is truly intractable. Given that every situation displays energy and movement, moment by moment, the only things in question are how fast and in what *direction* change occurs.

Having No Self

Similarly, seeing all things—including ourselves—as having no essential nature or identity means that we cannot claim anything to be inherently good or inherently bad. This makes it impossible for us either to be dogmatic about our own beliefs and values or to hold firm prejudices against those of others. In a very immediate fashion, it dissolves the grounds for the racial, ethnic, or religious stereotyping that underlies so much of contemporary social and political conflict. At the same time, it dissolves any possible reason for claiming that a person cannot change, that we simply are who we are. By seeing all things as *anatman*—literally, as having "no self"—we forfeit the basic conditions of maintaining chronic conflicts and opposition.

In later forms of Buddhism, the teaching of no-self was strongly allied with the practice of seeing all things as empty *(sunya)*—that is, as a relational pattern of interdependence. An analogy would be the relatively stable interference pattern that appears in a pond when two or more stones are dropped into its otherwise still water. The impact of each stone sends out a radiating set of waves. These sets of waves intersect at particular points on the surface of the pond, and an overall pattern of intersections emerges. Once the waves stop radiating from the points of impact, this pattern begins fading out and eventually disappears.

In the same way, everything in one's situation—including one's own self—emerges through the coming together of certain conditions. Things can be seen as having no essence or core because they actually consist of particular *patterns of relationship.* That is, nothing literally exists or stands apart from all others. For this reason, in later Buddhist usage, emptiness—the absence of any abiding, essential nature—is often equated with fullness. Far from signifying its privation, the emptiness of a thing consists in its unique way of bringing all other things into focus. Through each thing, all things join.

A good, concrete example is the way species relate within a sustainable ecosystem. Although it can appear competitive, a sustainable ecosystem is a space of mutual contributions. In it, each species offers some distinctive way of processing and circulating the resources of the system as a whole. In this way, they more or less directly contribute to the welfare of all the other species in the system.

Consider trees. As members of an ecosystem, trees depend on and are depended upon by many other species (some microscopic). In addition to mutual support with other living beings, trees depend on the balanced presence of soil, rainwater, sunlight, and gravity. In fact, they bring these into very unique patterns of relationship. But soil, water, sunlight, and gravity do not exist independently either. They can occur—literally, "flow together"—only on a planet circling a star at a suitable distance for water to take liquid form and with sufficient mass and atmospheric pressure to retain it. In turn, planets arise only in the presence of both deep gravitational wells and heavy matter of the sort produced in the hearts of very old stars. Stars arise only as parts of galaxies that are themselves parts of galactic families and so on. The conditions generating any particular tree have no known limit in space or time. Trees literally and uniquely gather into themselves the forces of the heavens and earth and tell one irreplaceable aspect of their shared history. Seeing all things as empty or having no self is to open ourselves to the unique ways in which they contribute to our nature and the meaning of our presence together.

Doing so, we begin realizing that what we have been referring to as "trees," "planets," "human beings," or "histories" are simply our personal editions of the total pattern of relationships that they focus. For a lab worker, a dog is just an experimental animal that must be treated with a specific amount of respect but that lives for the sole purpose of being subjected to tests that will advance human knowledge. For an only child, a dog can be a playmate, a friend, and even a member of the family. What we take a dog to be reflects our own values—the horizons of what we believe (or will allow) to be relevant.

The particulars of our experience are thus deeply conditioned by our values and intentions. Indeed, day-to-day experiences do not give complete pictures of one's situation but only extensively edited versions of it. Finally, they tell us more about ourselves—about our purposes and the horizons we set for what will count as relevant—than they do about the world as such. Seeing all things as empty is first to realize that what we take to be objects existing independently of ourselves are, in actuality, compounded or put together out of habitual patterns of relationship. Second, it is to free ourselves continuously from those habits.

Many of these habits are entirely personal in nature, reflecting our individual likes and dislikes. But because we are born into families and communities and cultures, many of the ways in which our ignorance is habitually patterned are "inherited." We are taught what things are and are not by parents, teachers, and friends but also by our culture more broadly. By appreciating the emptiness of all things, we become aware that the world we live in did not arise randomly, according to inherently fixed principles, or according to the purely objective operation of natural laws. Rather, it has taken shape in conformity with our likes and dislikes, according to our values, through our intentions, to meet our needs and desires. In Buddhist terms, our world is an expression of our karma.

THE TEACHING OF KARMA

The Buddhist teaching of karma invites us to see the shape of our life histories as corresponding with our own values and intentions. Conflicts we encounter are not to be seen—as was common in the Buddha's India—as simple and objective consequences directly caused by our own actions and the blind operations of universal moral law. Nor are they to be seen as a function of so-called natural law or mere chance. Rather, they are to be seen as reflecting ongoing and always situated tensions among our own values and aspirations, the patterns of our likes and dislikes, and the strength of our desires and dreams. Likewise, when things are "working out," this is to be seen as reflecting an overall consonance among our values, not "good luck" or some transcendently ordained fate. The teaching of karma asks us to see that we have (and share) responsibility for the direction in which things are headed. The meaning of our situation is always open to revision.

The Buddha most commonly talked about karma in terms of basic life orientations—either toward the chronic and intense trouble and suffering of samsara or toward liberation from these, nirvana. However, directing ourselves toward one or the other does not rest on an ability to *exert one's will independently* in shaping the world as we want. Karmically, the willful control of our circumstances brings about a life in which our circumstances seem only increasingly in need of (further) control. Instead, our capacity for revising our present situation rests on our seeing ourselves as not being independently existing beings but as thoroughly interdependent.

Seeing things karmically is to see our world as irreducibly dramatic. It is a world in which all things are not only factually but also meaningfully interdependent. Intentions and values not only matter, they are an irreducible part of how things come about. In strictly *factual* terms, a single microbe on a distant planet can make only an infinitesimal contribution to our life here on earth. It cannot alter the course of global warming or restore either local or global ecological health. But simply by being (even very distantly) present, it changes the meaning of our own place in the cosmos. It shows that life on earth is not a complete anomaly and that we are not ultimately alone. In this dramatic sense, a single microbe can make a world of difference.

In all Buddhist contexts, the teaching of karma is embedded in a cosmology that denies the simple finality of death. The term for a life of chronic trouble and suffering—"samsara"—literally refers to an unending and compulsive cycle of birth and death. In early forms of Buddhism, nirvana was often defined as a release from this compulsive cycle. For later Buddhists, liberation was not necessarily understood as marking freedom from the cycle of birth and death itself but only from its compulsive quality.

For the Vedic traditionalists living in the Buddha's India, death marked the departure of an eternal soul or life-essence (atman) from the physical body. Depending on the actions committed by this departed soul, it would either be restored to its origin in the universal Soul or be reborn in one of several types of body. It might reincarnate in human form. But it might also reincarnate in the form of an animal, a hungry ghost, a titan, or even a god. While Buddhism largely accepted this general cosmological schema and the presence of different birth realms, it also involved a rejection of some of its core premises. This entirely changed the meaning of "previous lives," "rebirth," and karma.

As seen in the teaching of the three marks, Buddhist practice involves undermining our assumption that there exists something like an individual or universal, eternal soul or self. Seeing all things as having no self is to see that there is literally nothing to be reborn or to receive a new body. Nor is there anything that could carry karma forward from one life to the next. Nevertheless, the Buddha spoke at great length about karma playing out over many lifetimes, even giving examples from his own "prior births." How is this to be understood?

When asked if the person who intentionally carries out an action is the very same person who will later experience its consequences, the Buddha replies that this would not be correct. Asked, then, if it is a different person who experiences the karmic results of an action, the Buddha again answers that this would not be correct. What he does affirm is that there is a connection between the actor and the one who experiences the consequences of an action. If there were no connection at all, he says, then there would be no point to Buddhist practice, no traveling of the Eightfold Path, and no chance of liberation.

If it is any consolation, this was no easier for most of the Buddha's Indian audiences to understand than it is for us today. The crucial question is how there can be karmic continuity if there is no essential and abiding self that persists over the course of not just one but many lifetimes. If the actor and the person experiencing the consequences of action are neither the same nor different, then what possible connection could they have?

As a way of responding, reconsider the metaphor of stones being tossed into a pond. In the course of our lives, we cast many stones. That is, we act intentionally, projecting our values decisively into our situation. Each one of these "stones" sets the pond's surface into vibration, creating a radiating set of waves that course outward and, eventually, rebound. The total pattern created by all these overlapping waves constitutes who we are as actors—our personalities. When waves strike and rebound off objects in the pond or bounce off the pond's edges, they reflect the shapes of those objects and of the pond itself and then alter or contribute to the overall pattern of who we are. These returning waves are the more or less immediate, experiential consequences of our actions.

Now, imagine that the border of this pond, our lived world, is a flexible membrane that separates it from other adjacent ponds. As the most powerful or persistent sets of waves—the carriers of our most powerful or persistent intentions and values—reach this membrane, they set it into motion. No water from our pond—none of our life substance—passes into the adjacent pond. No stone that is cast into our pond also falls into an adjacent one. Still, there appears in that other pond an interference pattern very much like the one appearing in our own. In that life, the same values, likes and dislikes, intentions, and desires will play out.

This is only a metaphor for how karma works. It will, like all analogies and metaphors, break down at some point. Nevertheless, it is useful to explore its implications. First, it is clear that we are not alone in casting stones into the pond and that "who we are" is influenced by what others do—their values and intentional activity. We are not present in our own lives as self-existing entities but as patterns of interdependence. Second, although there is continuity in the dramatic pattern of lived experience from life to life, no soul or bodily substance crosses over the barrier of death—the pond's bordering membrane. No self —no pattern of relational vibrations—is literally lifted from one pond and set into another. That is, the actors are not reincarnated. What connects a prior life to a present or future life are just patterns of meaningful relationship.

To press the dramatic metaphor, one can say that although the actors will change in each life, characters remain constant. Each life in a "birth series" is like a Shakespearean drama performed by different sets of actors in different cities who are always free to improvise changes in the course and meaning of the play. Our life stories are part of a continuum of "performances" in which shared and developing dramatic themes and values are embodied.

In the *Jataka Tales,* or birth stories of the Buddha, a continuing cast of characters plays the changing roles proper to each life. This dramatic ensemble—like an acting troupe that has been together for some time —is a special sort of family affair. Sometimes, the Buddha in his prior birth is a leading character who shows other members of the ensemble what it means to orient their interactions or drama toward liberation from trouble and suffering. In other birth stories, one of these other characters may take the lead as teacher or as father or as king. As a whole, the dramatic ensemble reaches a collective turning point in the life of Siddhartha Gautama. In this life, the entire group of karmic cohorts—the Buddha's foremost disciples, his father, his stepmother, his wife, his son, and so on—realize the meaning of irreversible, full awakening.

The Ecology of Awakening: The Diversity of Buddhist Paths

Buddhist practice aims at healing the wound of existence. It provides guidance for blazing a meaningful path out of the compulsive cycle of birth and death and the trouble and suffering that are inevitably a part of it. As such, Buddhist practice is always both a critique of self and a critique of culture. Although our individual values, intentions, and desires are central to our karma and the kind of life we experience, so are the broader values and patterns of conduct that we inherit from our culture.

In the Buddha's own life, for example, he often had to counter assumptions that seemed perfectly normal to people born into the culture of caste and gender bias that played such an important role in structuring Indian society. As he directed his students to travel and widely transmit the Dharma, he made it clear that they should not become attached to his exact words and style of discourse. Instead, he instructed them to adopt the local language to whatever extent possible and to speak to each audience in an appropriate way. In fact, a key characteristic of bodhisattvas, or "enlightening beings," is their manifestation of unlimited resources for responding to the specific—and, at times, peculiar—needs of an audience. Simply put, if suffering differs from person to person and from culture to culture, so must the healing response to suffering.

As Buddhist teachings spread out from northeast India into the rest of the Asian continent, they underwent significant interfusion with local cultures and belief systems. This fusion continues to take place as various forms of Buddhism reach the West. And so, although Thai Buddhism and Tibetan Buddhism both trace their origins to the original teachings of the Buddha, they are arguably as different as Christianity and Islam. And while both traditions respond, for example, to the contemporary world and the challenges of rapid economic and political globalization, they do so in distinctive ways.

Given this variation, it would be misleading to view the historical development of Buddhism in a linear fashion—either as a progressive evolution leading up to the present or as a regressive devolution in which the Buddha's original insights become increasingly obscured. Instead, it seems best to view Buddhist history as a countercultural

ecology of awakening. Contributing to this diverse ecological whole
are three main traditions, the Theravada, the Mahayana, and the
Vajrayana, each with many individual branches.

Each of these three "vehicles" (as they are often referred to in Buddhist circles) represents a unique pattern of response to the personal
and cultural problem of suffering. The Theravada takes the *arhat*, or
"saint," to be the ideal of personal development—a Buddhist practitioner who has realized the cessation of all entangling forms of thought
and action, and who has stopped making any karma that would continue to spin the wheel of birth and death. The saint has "cooled
down" or "blown out" all of those passions that compel us toward
conflict, cultivating instead unreserved compassion and loving-kind-
ness. Released from karmic and relational bondage, the saint leaves
samsara altogether at death. For the Theravada traditions, samsara
and nirvana *(nibbana)* are understood as radically distinct. They hold
that one can no more say where the saint goes after death than one can
say where a flame goes when it is blown out. Drawing on texts
recorded in the Pali language, the Theravada focuses on the historical
Buddha as teacher. Because they focused on personal release from suffering, these traditions were often disparagingly referred to by other
Buddhist lineages as the Hinayana, or "small (or lesser) vehicle."
Claiming, nevertheless, to represent the most direct inheritors of the
earliest forms of Buddhist thought and practice, Theravada traditions
are now found, for example, in Thailand, Burma, Laos, and Sri Lanka.

The Mahayana tradition takes the bodhisattva, or "enlightening
being," as the ideal of personal development—a Buddhist practitioner
who has vowed to continue cycling through birth and death until he
or she has participated in the liberation of all sentient beings. While
bodhisattvas have also dissolved the roots of bondage in this world,
they remain fully present in it. Released from contributory limits, they
have developed unlimited skill in improvising liberating responses to
the dilemmas of daily life. For the Mahayana, samsara and nirvana are
not distinct realms. Indeed, the tradition claims that not even a single
hair can be slipped between them—they are two sides of a single phe-
nomenon. Awakening is not a release from the world but rather realizing that this very world is already a buddha-realm in which all things
are doing the work of enlightenment. Mahayana teachings were orig-

inally recorded in the Sanskrit language and include teachings not only from the historical Buddha, but also from many other ahistorical buddhas and bodhisattvas. Although the roots of the Mahayana can be detected even in the earliest strata of Buddhist texts, this vehicle is most commonly thought to have begun flourishing between the first century B.C.E. and the first century C.E. It is now found, for example, in China, Japan, Korea, and Vietnam.

The Vajrayana tradition develops out of the Mahayana as an esoteric extension of its distinctive features. The ideal person is the spiritual adept who attains buddhahood in this very life and who is free even from "natural laws." Making use of tantric practices that transmute the energies of this world into forces for awakening, such adepts work to accelerate history or evolution in order to transform this world into a buddha-realm in which the nonduality of all things is utterly manifest. Vajrayana teachings are largely recorded in the Tibetan language, and the tradition places special emphasis on particular human teachers who, from life to life, carry on the work of awakening all beings, doing so as emanations of cosmic buddhas and bodhisattvas. The "diamond vehicle," as the Vajrayana is sometimes called, is generally thought to have arisen through a blending of Buddhism and Hindu tantric rituals and concepts in the fifth and sixth centuries C.E., flourishing most vividly on the Tibetan plateau from the ninth century onward. It is now found in Tibet, Bhutan, parts of Mongolia, and in the Tibetan diaspora centered in Dharamsala in northeast India.

To look at any of these three vehicles as they are practiced in Asia, but also in the West, is to see that Buddhism not only changes the indigenous culture when it is assimilated, it is also changed by that culture. In general, it can be said that there are two phases (often occurring simultaneously) in this process of assimilation that weds Buddhist and indigenous values in a relationship conducive to awakening: accommodation and advocacy. Understanding them is crucial to the story of Chan and the advent of truly Chinese forms of Buddhism.

During the phase of accommodation, Buddhist concepts and practices are incorporated into the indigenous cultural framework, and the original system of these concepts and practices is opened in such a way as to accommodate some important local concepts and practices.

As an example, Korean Buddhist temples have altars devoted to spirit forces from native shamanism that have been "converted" by Buddhism and serve as protectors of the faith. This kind of accommodation is crucial if Buddhism is to perform a truly countercultural function—that is, if it is to criticize and revise that culture from within. Otherwise, it will remain an entirely alien set of practices in conflict with local traditions. As such, it could never do the buddha-work of karmically resolving trouble or suffering.

A major part of the phase of accommodation pivots on the translation of Buddhist teachings and texts into local languages. But that alone is not enough. For example, Christian, Islamic, and Judaic texts have been translated into Chinese since at least the Tang dynasty with very little sustained impact on the religious or spiritual culture of the Chinese people. While there are Chinese Christians, Muslims, and Jews, they have always been very much in the minority and are largely viewed as "ethnic" in nature. They have not—with the tragic exception of the Taiping movement—been considered fully Chinese. Because Buddhism does not offer absolute truths about the way the world is, but rather strategies for resolving trouble and suffering as we experience them, it must always begin with an acceptance of this situation as it is taking place. Refusing to do so is to refuse to be in a position truly to help others or ourselves to revise the meaning of our presence together.

As Buddhism moves into a new cultural sphere, it acknowledges that the local culture and the personality structures that it sponsors embody values that to some extent have "worked." Buddhist spirituality entails first making room for these indigenous resources and then opening them in new directions. This second phase can be referred to as one of advocacy.

In this phase, Buddhist concepts and practices are used both to assess indigenous resources for responding to the problem of suffering/trouble and to enhance them concretely. Ideally, Buddhist advocacy is not a matter of comprehensively supplanting indigenous value systems and rituals but rather of selectively supplementing them. This process depends on improvising personal and cultural narratives that are recognized by the indigenous population as complementing, and not conflicting, with their own. When fully successful, as it was in

China by the ninth or tenth century C.E., the transition from accommodation to advocacy makes possible an internal and yet fully Buddhist countercultural critique.

The Historical Spread of Buddhism into China and the Birth of Chinese Buddhism

Buddhism first entered China roughly two thousand years ago and for several centuries had a relatively modest impact on Chinese society. By the eighth century, however, Buddhism had become so integral a part of the Chinese way of life that somewhere between five hundred thousand and seven hundred thousand men and women were ordained as Buddhist monks or nuns—roughly one out of every eighty-five people in a country of approximately fifty million. So thoroughly did Buddhism become infused into Chinese culture that it came to be seen by many Chinese as a native tradition alongside Confucianism and Daoism—China's great indigenous religious and philosophical systems. Like different peaks in a mountain range, these three teachings came eventually to be seen by many as at root one.

Initially, the spread of Buddhism through China took place through new forms of ritual and therapeutic conduct imported by Buddhist meditative adepts and through the translation of Indian Buddhist texts into Chinese. China and India are often thought of as two virtually autonomous cultural spheres, separated by both the tallest mountain range in the world and impassably dense jungles. But already in the first century C.E., fairly substantial trade and cultural diffusion were taking place through the mountain passes of Central Asia controlled by the Kusana Empire and over the northern and southern Silk Roads that skirted the Talka Makan desert basin. Along these trade routes, joined at Kashgar in the west and at Dunhuang in the east, were vibrant centers of commerce and learning where Chinese, Indian, and Iranian civilizations blended and through which a continuous stream of Buddhist lay merchants and itinerant monks passed on their way into Han dynasty China.

For some time, the Chinese viewed Buddhism strictly as a "barbarian" religion that merited little direct attention except as a cultural curiosity. But as the later Han dynasty started coming apart at the seams, increasing numbers of aristocrats and members of the imperial court turned to Buddhism as an alternative religious technology—an alternate framework for making sense out of and forestalling (if not reversing) the imminent collapse of the empire. For at least half a millennium, a core premise of Chinese politics had been that the authority to rule was founded on the "mandate of heaven"—a mandate visible to all because it was "sealed" by the union and harmony of Chinese society itself. The apparent failure of the court to maintain the empire's unity and vitality proved that there was a threat that heaven's mandate would be withdrawn not only from the ruling elite but from its Confucian and Daoist ritual technologies as well. This was a powerful incentive to seek out other systems of value and ritual.

The Han dynasty eventually fell in 220 C.E. Throughout the ensuing three centuries of disunity, China's educated elite made deepening use of Buddhist concepts, rituals, and meditative techniques, and sponsored the building of monasteries and shrines. In this way, it was effectively insured that Buddhist values and practices were incorporated into China's enduring cultural body. Teams of native and foreign scholars were commissioned to carry out massive translation projects, and it quickly became apparent that China had so far gained access to only a tiny fraction of the Buddhist canon. Text-gathering missions were sent to India, Chinese Buddhist scholars began the task of sorting and organizing the vast body of literature, and there evolved a rigorously academic commentarial tradition centered on Buddhist thought and practice.

It was during this period that Buddhist scholasticism in China first matured. Study groups formed around Central Asian and Indian texts and teachers from both Theravada and Mahayana traditions, though the latter were in much greater number. Among the most important of these were groups centered on treatises from the Madhyamika and Yogacara schools of Indian Buddhist thought. The former came closest to being an identifiable and coherent school of Chinese thought, the Sanlun. In addition, groups formed around key Mahayana texts, most prominently the *Lotus Sutra* and the *Nirvana Sutra.* By the seventh and eighth centuries, the recitation of such key sutras, translated into Chinese, became an important part of village-level Buddhist observance and was associated with both vegetarian feasts and ritual offerings for the benefit of family and clan ancestors.

At the same time, interest in rigorous meditation discipline was growing. In the earliest centuries of Buddhist transmission into China, ruling aristocracies were content to bring Buddhist meditation masters into their fold in the hope of benefiting from their extraordinary perceptual abilities and skills in both physical and psychic healing. By the fourth century, however, communities of meditation practitioners formed around such Buddhist adepts as the Kuchean miracle worker Fotudeng. In part, this trend seems to have been a function of prevalent Chinese convictions that purely intellectual knowledge is at best incomplete. Any true understanding is necessarily embodied and practically demonstrated. From at least the sixth century, it was possible for committed Buddhists—both ordained and lay—to participate in one-month and three-month-long meditation retreats, using a variety of techniques ranging from breath-focused mindfulness to invocations of the Buddha's name, the repetition of energy phrases or mantra, and visualization.

This combination of textual study and meditation practice laid the foundation for the first truly Chinese schools of Buddhism that would flower over a three-hundred-year period from the sixth through ninth centuries: Tiantai, Huayan, Qingtu, and Chan. These four schools, each in its own unique fashion, represent the mature fruit of Buddhist accommodation and advocacy in China. Although differing in distinctive ways in their approach to conceiving and practicing Buddhist spirituality—differences that will be addressed in modest detail in a later chapter—each of these schools ultimately shared a belief that all beings, without exception, have or express buddha-nature and are thus candidates for awakening or enlightenment.

As China moved toward reconsolidation under the Sui in 589, however, very real tensions developed between indigenous cultural canons and their imported Buddhist counterparts. The first large-scale purge of Buddhism took place in 446, and major imperially sanctioned persecutions took place again in 574 and 842–845. In this last exercise of imperial authority over Buddhism, the Tang emperor Wuzong forced over a quarter of a million monks and nuns back into society at large and destroyed nearly five thousand temples and forty-thousand shrines across the country. While doctrinal conflicts between Buddhism and either Confucianism or Daoism were often cited in justifying such persecutions, more important perhaps was the economic impact of Buddhism's tax-free religious status.

The unified China of the Sui (589–617) and Tang (617–907) is often depicted as exhibiting unparalleled cultural creativity, cosmopolitanism, and political stability. China extended its borders to include very nearly its present-day land area. The Grand Canal was built to connect China's major waterways, making it possible to develop the first truly unified imperial economy and to fund major overseas trade missions to Southeast and South Asia and overland missions to Central Asia and the Near East.

The development of global commerce brought familiar consequences: a growing income gap between wealthy and poor; the emergence of a strong merchant middle class; the rise of fashions in clothing, art, and literature; and cultivated tastes for foreign goods. By the seventh century, the Tang capital, Chang'an, had become the largest and most cosmopolitan city in the world. One million people lived within its walls and another million in the immediately surrounding area, a sizable proportion of which was non-Chinese. In the city were hundreds of Confucian, Daoist, and Buddhist temples and shrines but also Manichean, Nestorian Christian, and Zoroastrian temples and churches.

China's new and distant borders were, however, hard to defend. The logistics of moving armies numbering in the hundreds of thousands as far as two thousand miles during a single military campaign required high levels of taxation throughout the empire. Border clashes were common, internal protests were increasingly strident, and the cultural tensions associated with maintaining imperial unity over a land area nearly four times that of Western Europe became increasingly clear. These tensions reached critical mass over the decade from 755 to 764, when a combination of rebellion and famine left two out of every three people in the country either dead or missing, cutting the official population from 53 million to only 17 million. To put this tragedy in stark historical perspective, the global civilian and military casualties associated with World War II numbered between 38 and 50 million out of a world population of 2.5 billion—roughly one out of every fifty people on the planet.

It is impossible to overestimate the utterly devastating effect such a catastrophic loss of life must have had on the spiritual resources of the Chinese people. It was in this highly charged and spiritually distraught environment that Chan emerged as a distinctive approach to the practice of Buddhism. The sixth and seventh centuries had already witnessed a sharp rise in the material resources expended on building Buddhist temples, monasteries, and shrines, casting Buddhist statues, and crafting ritual objects and clothing. This expense was borne on the belief that offerings made to the Buddhist community in this life would benefit donors and their families in lives to come. The fervor with which the Buddhist faithful made such offerings grew with alarming rapidity. By the eighth century, the overall capital and labor—not to mention spiritual reliance—that was flooding into the Buddhist community reached such high levels that an imperial edict written in 707 estimated that 70 to 80 percent of the total wealth of the empire was untaxed and in Buddhist hands.

This accumulation of wealth resulted in a series of imperial proscriptions against donations to Buddhism. It also triggered ongoing and widespread criticism of the gap between Buddhism's official profession of freedom from materialist attachments and its de facto willingness to accumulate wealth. It is only in light of these historical conditions that the consolidation of a characteristically Chan form of Buddhism can be properly understood. Just as crucial, however, were the roles played by China's indigenous spiritual, religious, and philosophical traditions—particularly Confucianism and Daoism. There is no adequate understanding of Chan without taking into account the complex accommodations that took place between these native traditions and the Buddhist teachings and practices that arrived from beyond China's borders over three-quarters of a millennium.

CHAPTER 2

Differences in Indian and Chinese Cultural Contexts

Buddhism aims at resolving suffering. Because of this, it does not come in any universal, "one size fits all" form. As suffering is never generic, neither are its resolutions. What we suffer and how are inseparable from where and when we were born, the cultures we call our own, and the choices and values that have helped make us who we are. Granted this, Buddhist practice involves critically challenging both our cultural inheritances and the dispositions that shape our unique and individual approaches to being human.

These are not challenged because they are inherently bad—that is, because in every possible situation they have and will always make for trouble. The personal boundaries that define who we take ourselves to be can be seen as developing (at least in part) as natural defenses. They make it clear, for example—as much to ourselves as to others—where actions become transgressions. Our sense of individuality and independence often tends to obscure and even deny our interdependence with all things—a form of ignorance that leaves us open to both unexpected and chronic trouble. It can also be seen as playing a role in helping us believe in our freedom to stop suffering and to solve our own problems. Likewise, our cultural inheritances include belief systems, social institutions, technologies, arts, and rituals that (at least partly) originated in practical concerns for both personal and communal security and comfort. As such, they embody a history of responses to both actual and possible troubles and crises.

When Buddhist practice challenges our sense of independent self-existence and our cultural inheritances, it is challenging specific and ultimately ineffective strategies for resolving suffering. Although we—as individuals and as cultures—have developed ways of dealing with trouble and suffering, they often just replace one form of trouble with another. Automotive technology, for example, solved many transportation problems. But over time it has so changed our lived environment that many cities have such toxic levels of air pollution that greenhouse gases now threaten the health of the earth's biosphere as a whole. Such self-defeating "cures" are often very hard to recognize from the inside. Alcohol and drug abusers, for instance, often insist that there is nothing wrong with their habits. Against all objective evidence, they believe that alcohol and drugs are effective, even if only short-term, solutions to their problems.

The Buddhist aim of skillfully resolving trouble or suffering involves becoming intimate with such strategies. Intimacy takes place in a space between the purely subjective and the purely objective. Within that space even those practices that seem most natural and successful—for example, caste systems, slavery, gender discrimination, or religious intolerance—can be opened to challenge. The rise of truly Chinese Buddhism marks the achievement of just this sort of intimacy. And, as an exemplary form of Chinese Buddhism, the Chan tradition is best approached as a corrective for locally prevailing strategies for personally and communally understanding and responding to suffering.

It is not possible to appreciate Chinese Buddhism and the distinctive spirituality of Chan fully without some understanding of the differences between indigenous, non-Buddhist Indian and Chinese approaches to the end of suffering. These differences can be brought into summary focus by looking at the cultural stories that serve as templates relating persons and their suffering with the order of the cosmos. Nowhere, perhaps, are these stories as starkly at odds as when expressing the meaning of death and dying.

The Disparate Meanings of Being Dead in India and China

While all human societies have developed ways of understanding death and of honoring the dead, India and China evolved very elaborate, and very different, conceptual and ritual systems for doing so. In India, the dominant cultural narrative about death involved funeral rituals that placed strict limits on grieving. The open expression of grief by family members and friends was thought to make it hard—perhaps even impossible—for the dead fully to sever their worldly ties. Only by doing so could the soul (atman) of the dead person achieve final release into identity with the universal Atman—the divine ground of all things. Failing this, the dead would continue to be reborn in bodies and life circumstances determined by the moral quality of their actions over the course of their recently ended lives. Because each person's true self or essence was understood as identical to the universal Atman, each rebirth was understood as yet another lapse into mistaken identity.

The traditional Indian cremation ritual ended with pulverizing the bones of the dead person and scattering this final powder and other ashes. Symbolically, this act announced the departed soul's freedom from any lasting connection with the people and places it had begun to leave behind. Ideally, this freedom is complete, immediate, and permanent. Then the soul is fully restored into the unity of limitless consciousness, existence, and bliss that is its own most profound truth. For those who have lived less than ideal lives, however, this will not be the case. Because of the karma created over the course of their lives, they will be obliged—at some point in space and time—to be reborn and to resume interactions with others as apparently separate and often contrary beings.

Indian ancestor worship aimed at encouraging the soul to continue its migration out of this world, putting an end to its mistaken identification with a physical body, the life circumstances surrounding it, and the necessity of continued separation and suffering. In the mainstream Indian cultural narrative, suffering truly ends only through achieved reunion with the unlimited, pure presence that is Brahman—a final break in the continuity of all relationships through the realization of absolute existence.

In China, the dominant cultural narrative about death and ancestral worship was almost completely opposite. The funeral ritual involved the display of intense and long-lasting grief, especially by the dead person's children and closest relatives. After burial of the body, regular offerings of food and drink were made to the dead as a way of insuring that they would remain "in the home" along with other family members. As elders, the dead were accorded great respect and remained prominently in the midst of their family or clan. In fact, ancestors were ritually consulted in every major decision-making situation.

The mainstream Indian conviction was that each person has a single, permanent soul. The Chinese were inclined to allow that we are each a gathering of several kinds of "spirit" or subtle forms of energy that leave the body at death and return to their separate and proper places in the cosmos. The truth of a person is not, however, given in any one of these departing spirits or in their shared essence. Indeed, they can be seen as natural elements that help compose us much as wood, metal, glue, and bone are elements in the composition of a guitar or a violin. Our true nature as persons consists of a unique body of relationships that can be nurtured, extended, and refined. For the Chinese, being truly human is achieved through cultivating concretely lived (especially familial and social) relationships. Suffering does not end through release from every sort of binding intercourse with others but with the realization of continuously correct relationships.

Lying behind these very different stories about death and what it means to be a person are strikingly opposed conceptions of order. In the dominant Vedic tradition of India, change and multiplicity ultimately are understood as illusions. The order of the cosmos is given as eternal and universal, and suffering is finally a result of not being aware of our ultimate identity with the essence of this order. In China, change was not understood as an illusion but as the basic condition of all things. Thus the ancient classic the *Yijing* represents the order of the cosmos as a "familial" process of generation-like transformations that is incomplete in the absence of the unexpected. For the Chinese, order did not imply absolute unity but rather an ongoing harmony of differences and deference.

The Vedic Indian cosmos—not entirely unlike the Christian one—can be pictured as a closed circle: the origin of all things is, finally, identical with their end. The Chinese world, by contrast, suggests an open spiral or spring that has neither a clear beginning nor a clear end. Confucius—arguably China's most influential sage—thus claimed that it is not the Dao, or pattern of the cosmos, that extends what it means to be human but humans who extend the Dao. Creativity, for the Chinese, is part of the way things always are.

Not surprisingly, while Indian philosophy and religious culture grappled with a deep tension between the absolute One (Atman or Brahman) and the apparent multiplicity of individual souls, in China a comparable tension played out between the cultivated sage and the uncultivated commoner. In India, human self-realization and the end of suffering finally meant release from all natural and social forms of relatedness. In China, they meant realizing exemplary skill in achieving and maintaining appropriate natural and human relations.

The Complementary Streams of Early Chinese Religiousness: Confucianism and Daoism

From at least the fourth or fifth century B.C.E., there were two main strategies for doing so: Confucianism and Daoism. The best evidence suggests that these traditions emerged on substantially common ground and diverged only over a period of several centuries during the late Zhou and early Han dynasties. For the purpose of understanding Buddhist accommodation and advocacy in China, they are of crucial concern.

Surrounding and in many ways interpenetrating these relatively well-defined traditions, there also existed bodies of popular practice that were linked by no clear doctrines or institutions but that nevertheless formed a shared heritage of members of both common and elite society. Many of these practices have remained remarkably resilient for over two millennia and continue to play a part in the cultural life of China—for example, those comprising mortuary rites, New Year's celebrations, the appeasing of restless ghosts, and the consultation of spirit mediums or shamans. These practices all center on calling attention to and properly attending the complex relationships linking the living community with the communities of the spirit realm and their cosmic context. Because humans, ghosts, spirits, and gods were all understood and treated as equally "natural"—none, that is, being understood in the Western sense as supernatural or beyond nature—they were also seen as part of an overarching cosmic society throughout which the same basic principles and laws applied. Thus the spirit realm and gods came to be seen as organized in the same bureaucratic fashion as the human realm and susceptible to the same kinds of influences.

These bodies of practice thus formed (and continue to form) the basis of what might be referred to as Chinese popular religion—a religion aimed at respecting, revering, and (when necessary) restoring the natural social harmony of the cosmos. As such, they not only provided a broad religious background against which Confucianism, Daoism, and (later) Buddhism were understood and practiced by most Chinese, they also (at times) provided a shared space for expressing nonelite or minority concerns and norms. Because of their amorphous nature, however, and their tacit inclusion in all forms of Chinese religiousness, I will limit my discussion of early Chinese strategies for insuring human flourishing in a world not (at least, not entirely) of our own making to those clearly articulated in Confucianism and Daoism.

CONFUCIANISM

When Confucius was born in the sixth century B.C.E., China was in a state of self-conscious decline. The Zhou ruling family that had supplanted the last and most decadent of the Shang kings in the eleventh century B.C.E. had itself fallen into both political and moral straits. China—the so-called Middle or Centered Kingdom—had disintegrated into seemingly endless and overlapping struggles for authority, with no clear central leadership or moral axis. Translated into the daily experience of the people, this meant uncertain supplies of food, lack of security, the disruption of the family, and the kinds of turbulent social relations that provided room for advantage to be taken by those least inclined to do so benevolently.

A well-read scholar and hopeful political advisor, Confucius found in the recorded acts and intentions of the founders of the Zhou a coherent and comprehensive strategy for responding to personal, social, and political turbulence and decline—a method for restoring settled and harmoniously flourishing community. His teachings—recorded by his students and collected in the text known as the *Analects*—centered on ritual conduct *(li)* and the cultivation of authoritative personhood *(ren)*. The dialogues and anecdotes that make up the *Analects* do not treat ritual conduct as empty habit or custom. Instead, rituals were understood as situation-specific, concrete patterns of human interaction through which the seminal insights of Chinese culture and civilization are actively conserved. In this sense, ritual conduct provides regular opportunities for directly embodying ancestral wisdom.

The *Analects* also make clear, however, that ritual conduct, or *li*, is not just a matter of going through culturally prescribed motions. It involves actively appropriating ancestral wisdom to one's immediate situation. A strong analogy obtains between this sense of ritual and the divinatory function of the *Yijing*, or *Book of Changes*—one of the ancient classics with which Confucius is intimately associated. The skeleton of the main text is made up of sixty-four six-line diagrams and imagistic descriptions of their composition. In the great commentary appended to this main text, these sixty-four hexagrams are described as models of common situational changes. These hexagrams can yield practical insight into the dynamics of one's present and future circumstances, but only when activated by one's own sustained awareness. Similarly, Confucian *li* will only yield social harmony when activated by *ren* in one's own immediate circumstances.

It might be thought that Confucius would have expended a great deal of effort in detailed description of such an important quality. But, in fact, he avoided giving any explicit definition of *ren*. From the examples he cites and the way he characterizes its importance, it is clear that *ren* marks a profound qualitative shift in how we conduct ourselves as human beings. When ritual conduct is carried out with *ren*, it is like hearing a virtuoso pianist giving an inspired performance of a Mozart concerto. Although many pianists can play the concerto, only the virtuoso makes the music come so fully alive that everyone present is moved by it, gathered into a spell of intensely shared appreciation.

Indeed, the effectiveness of ritually embodying *ren* or authoritative personhood was thought capable of reaching almost magical levels. Confucius maintained, for example, that political order could be effected in the absence of any overt actions because a sage ruler need only make himself respectful and take up his position in the ritually prescribed direction for his kingdom to order itself. So deeply rooted was this belief in the force of authoritative personhood that, in the Confucian world, social and political disunity and disruption were understood as signs of rulers who had lost their commanding presence, who no longer manifested *ren*. When they apparently had lost the mandate to mediate between heaven and earth and order their realm, the authority of such rulers could legitimately be challenged and overthrown.

Underlying this view was a sense of the world as a space of sympathetic resonance in which all things are intimately (and not only externally) related. Much as a vibrating tuning fork will set the strings of a guitar in sympathetic motion and vice versa, all things in the world are continuously adjusting to one another, even in the absence of overt contact. Thus, a calm leader in a time of crisis can settle a turbulent crowd, and a properly disposed people can avert natural disaster. By the second century B.C.E., this sense of the intrinsic relatedness of all things was formalized in a system of correlative thinking that linked orders of all scales and degrees of complexity, both human and natural.

For Confucius, the person who is *ren* is "authoritative" in the sense of carrying forward the best of a tradition. But he or she must also be capable of authoring that tradition anew, extending it qualitatively, and suiting it to the needs of the time. When *li* are conducted with *ren*, ancestral wisdom is not only actively embodied, but deepened and increased. Only in this way can ritual conduct continue to harmonize the situations in which it occurs. Only then will everyone present be drawn into practical and emotional consonance.

Confucian spirituality and its answer to the problem of personal and cultural continuity and flourishing consists of wedding *li* and *ren*—a wedding of culturally regulated patterns of ritual conduct with authoritative character and benevolent intent. A response to the breakdown of the world order linking the celestial, the human, and the natural, it is a tradition of human-focused spirituality for which creativity means the exemplary extension of historical precedent.

Although Confucius failed to find an influential position in the royal court or a wide audience for his commitments to conserving cultural insights, over time his "way of learning" would come to form the basic state ideology of a unified China and a central axis of China's intellectual canon.

DAOISM

Over the centuries that the Confucian tradition was consolidated, many dissenting perspectives arose. The most important and long-lived of these was the "School of the Way," or Daoism. Tradition has it that this distinctive approach to realizing harmony among the celestial, human, and natural realms was first articulated by a hermit-sage, Laozi, living at about the same time as Confucius and later refined and deepened by Zhuangzi in the fourth century B.C.E. But this tradition was itself a rather late development. The texts attributed to these Daoist progenitors—the *Daodejing* and the *Zhuangzi*—were classed under separate philosophical headings even throughout much of the Han dynasty. The former, after all, was ostensibly a mystically inflected treatise on proper statecraft; the latter, a complex collection of anecdotes, stories, and philosophical dialogues that patently argued for a quietist withdrawal from official life. Indeed, it was not until late in the second century (approximately 120 B.C.E.) that they were linked as core texts for a School of the Way.

The association was not, however, ungrounded. Both texts openly criticized the championing of cultural norms, ritual practice, and social hierarchy that were central to the then developing Confucian Way. For inspiration, they reached back to a period before Chinese historical memory when all things existed in spontaneously realized and maintained harmony—a preimperial chaos or undifferentiated wholeness. Not surprisingly, perhaps, these twin streams of Daoism fully merged and underwent a remarkable rise in prominence with the demise of the Han dynasty as China lapsed into what some believed was necessary and creative chaos.

Like Confucianism, Daoism was not solely a philosophical system. In an interesting historical accident, by the early third century B.C.E., perhaps because the *Daodejing* had been drafted into the service of Legalist thinkers arguing against the Confucian model of statecraft, Laozi came to be allied with Huangdi, the Yellow Emperor, who was said to have brought humankind not only military, magical, and medical arts, but also statecraft modeled on objective patterns in nature, not subjective morality. Thus, in spite of the *Zhuangzi*'s explicit denunciation of the Yellow Emperor, late-Han Daoism came to be associated with medicines, magic, spirit travel, and alchemy—an association that persisted in and became a driving force of the religious dimension of Daoism that developed from the second century C.E. onward.

Religious Daoism grew steadily throughout the period between the Han dynasty's fall and the reunification of China under the Sui and was clearly a response to the political and social turbulence characteristic of those centuries of disunity. Beginning with the tradition of the Way of the Celestial Masters, religious Daoism developed through a series of revelatory communications between the divine realm of immortals and humans, with each claiming to subsume and extend prior revelations. As systems of religious practice, all included relatively strict moral codes, vows of abstinence, visualization-based meditations, and the use of chemical elixirs that (in combination) would lead to the attainment of immortality.

Philosophical and religious Daoism are important, complexly interwoven, and yet undeniably different expressions of Chinese cultural sensibilities. In terms of the Chinese accommodation of Buddhism and the framing of Chinese Buddhist advocacy, however, it is the values and strategic commitments of the philosophical stream of Daoism that were most important. As it emerged at the end of the Han, philosophical Daoism insisted on according with the natural patterning of things *(dao)* through a powerful focusing of spontaneity.

The term *"dao"* is among the most important in Chinese culture. Often it is translated as "way" or "the Way." But when used as a verb, its root meanings include "leading forth," "speaking," "guiding," and "to blaze a trail." As a noun, it means "path," "a way (of doing things)," "art," and "teachings." *"Dao"* also means being true to how things go, fully going along with the patterned changes that make up the world. For Laozi and Zhuangzi, *"dao"* meant both the way each thing consists of a unique pattern of changes and the way the patterns of each of the world's myriad things are connected with all others.

Thus, a horse has a particular *dao* that includes eating grasses and grains, galloping across wide open spaces, and accepting the friendship and instructions of human beings. No other animal has precisely this way of being. At the same time, it is a way that only makes sense given the ways of all other things. Horses' long legs and powerful strides correspond with the need to outrun fleet-footed predators.

Their hooves correspond with their needs for both crossing difficult terrain and defending themselves. Their teeth are suited to crushing and milling hard grains. In contemporary scientific terms, organisms and their environments together make up an ecological whole—a seamless and self-sustaining way of things.

As each of the world's myriad things accords with its unique *dao*— its pattern of contributing to the whole—it holds open a path for the free circulation of energy *(qi)* from and back into the overall pattern or Dao of the cosmos. To accord with one's *dao* is to be wholly transparent and unhindered. According to Zhuangzi, "When energy *(qi)* circulates freely, the ten thousand things take care of themselves." That is, when the way of things *(dao)* is unobstructed, each thing is consonant with all other things. Harmony naturally and continuously prevails. Although each thing is a distinctive focusing of this circulatory process, it is fully continuous with all others.

Instead of carefully rehearsing culturally regulated rituals as a way of countering the conditions of our human suffering, the Daoist tradition recommends letting go of any and all principles and certainties. In the unending transformation of things and events, insisting on such regularities is simply to deny our continuity with all things. Thus, in one of Zhuangzi's most famous vignettes, he wakes from a dream in which he was a butterfly dreaming about being Zhuangzi. In the very next moment, however, Zhuangzi realizes that he really has no way of telling if he is a man dreaming of himself as a butterfly or a butterfly dreaming of itself as a man. Trying to insist on one or the other view as true is finally just an obstruction of the transformation of things and the free and easy circulation of *qi*. That is the root of all our suffering.

For the (philosophical) Daoist tradition, there is no need for "cultivation" if we want to stop suffering and ease ourselves of trouble. We need only minimize our reliance on artifacts and artifice. For Laozi, the ideal society is one in which a wide array of technologies are available, but people seldom make use of them. In such a society, there would be no need for values like authoritativeness *(ren)* and justice, or for ancient customs and formal learning. These are deemed necessary only when the natural way of things *(dao)* has been blocked or interrupted. In the Daoism of Laozi and Zhuangzi, practice is oriented toward realizing unprincipled knowledge, objectless desire, and nonassertive action. Having realized these aims, we can make our way spontaneously, in free and easy wandering.

If the Confucian ideal person is the sage-ruler stationed in a bureaucratically organized and ritually focused government, the ideal Daoist is a sage-recluse who passes among us as if cloud-hidden, whereabouts unknown. For such persons, there is no question of maintaining continuity in the face of unexpected changes by holding onto the wisdom of the past or the genius of bygone cultural heroes. Daoist sages are like jazz musicians soloing with unconstrained immediacy over the changes of a driving rhythm section. They insure constancy by eliminating all their preconceived notions and habits. Realizing virtuosic flexibility, their method is one of unobstructed, adaptive improvisation. Although their presence may be pivotal in bringing about social harmony, they will not be noticed, blending in naturally with the ways of all things.

Confucian humanism and Daoist naturalism mark the polar extremes of traditional China's own strategies for understanding the human place in the cosmos, for articulating the meaning of cosmic harmony, and for responding to suffering or trouble. The Buddha referred to his teachings as a Middle Path between two extremes in the traditional Indian worldview. On the one side were Vedic commitments to both sacrificial rituals and the existence of an eternal absolute. On the other side were materialist denials of both the efficacy of ritual sacrifice and the existence of any absolute or eternal soul. In China, the development of fully Chinese Buddhism eventually involved blazing a similarly responsive Middle Path between Confucianism's humanistic *li* and Daoism's cosmic/natural *dao*, between conduct demonstrating authoritative personhood and conduct marked by free and easy spontaneity.

CHAPTER 3
Early Developments in Chinese Buddhism

The turning point of the Buddha's quest for a solution to the problem of suffering came with his insight into the interdependence of all things. Discerning a middle way between the twin barbs of "is" and "is-not"—a way toward healing the wound of existence—he described this insight as like coming across a "lost and forgotten city" in deep jungle, almost entirely overgrown and hidden from view.

The metaphor suggests seeing Buddhist liberation as a process of recovery or restoration. Rather than marking a discovery, the opening of an entirely new dimension, or a literal transcendence of all that has come before, liberation entails personally restoring a kind of presence that has for a long time been missing or neglected. As Buddhism becomes fully Chinese and Chan emerges as one of its exemplary forms, this understanding of liberation as recovering one's own original nature becomes explicit and authoritative.

To explain the meaning of his crucial insight, the Buddha often made use of the twelvefold chain of interdependent arising. This teaching device directs attention toward patterns of mutual conditioning taking place among the diverse aspects of one's personal makeup and life circumstances. Depending on how these patterns are directed as a whole, we move either in the direction of further suffering and trouble or toward their meaningful resolution. This total system is our way of becoming both in and of the world.

Classical discussions of this teaching device often focused on three of the twelve links as particularly crucial turning points. Extending the Buddha's metaphor, these links can be thought of as the three main gates into the recovered city of the Middle Way—three definitive openings of our presence with all things. If our presence as a whole is oriented in the direction of samsara or further suffering and trouble, these gates appear as ignorance, habit formation, and clinging desires. When it is oriented, instead, in the direction of nirvana or the meaningful resolution of all suffering and trouble, then these same gates manifest as wisdom, attentive virtuosity, and moral clarity. The early history of Buddhism in China can be seen as a process of gradually framing these gates in distinctive and yet culturally Chinese terms.

In India, a great many of the Buddha's earliest recorded teachings were directed toward dissolving the commitments his audiences had to valuing permanence over change, their belief in the independent existence of the soul or self, and the supposed availability of a perspective (that of the universal Atman or Brahman) from which the entire world is simply bliss. In China, although such teachings were also circulated, they did not play as controversially or importantly as in Indian cultural contexts. From earliest times, Chinese culture already assumed that change was the very nature of things and not an illusion that needed to be somehow overcome. Likewise, it tended to view all things in terms of dispositions and relationships rather than essential characteristics. A particular animal is not a horse because it possesses some ideal horse essence or form but because it conducts itself in a horselike way under most (if not all) circumstances. Finally, when Buddhism first arrived in China, there was no tradition of anything like an original garden of Eden or a future heavenly paradise.

This consonance between many of Buddhism's central teachings and traditional Chinese culture was a major factor in their rapid, mutual accommodation. Indeed, without such readily apparent consonance, Buddhism would not likely have been able to find sufficient accommodation in China to perform its countercultural function. Instead, with its inclination toward celibate monasticism and its insistence on seeing the Buddha—and not any king or other worldly leader, even the Chinese emperor—as highest authority, Buddhism would likely have remained a foreign religion. The phase of critical advocacy might never have fully flourished.

As it happened, however, Buddhist thought and practice opened new spaces into which the spiritual dispositions of Confucianism and Daoism could be selectively extended. This development was deeply appealing in the centuries following the collapse of the Han dynasty and China's disintegration into short-lived confederations facing continuous threats of chaos. As China moved toward unity under the Sui and Tang dynasties, Buddhism was looked to not only for individual solace, but also for new values and strategies with which to undertake statecraft, define authority, and bring about communal continuity and excellence. Buddhism gradually shifted into stressing its differences from China's native traditions, advocating its own *dao*—the Middle Path—as both more advanced and complete than those of Confucianism and Daoism. The rhetorical effect of this shift toward emphasizing Buddhism's competitive advantages reached a functional apogee in the late Tang dynasty.

A crucial precondition for such open and full advocacy of Buddhism was a fundamental reframing of the grounds for Buddhist authority—a move away from Indian texts and teachings from the past to those of contemporary Chinese-born Buddhists. A brief account of this process will shed useful light on the cultural precedents for the conception and growth of Chan and its unprecedented and iconoclastic approach to opening the liberating gates of wisdom, attentive virtuosity, and moral clarity.

Texts and Contexts: The Phase of Accommodation

For Buddhism to function as an extension or alternative to China's native forms of spirituality, it had first to be brought into the lifeworld of Chinese culture and society. Daoism was particularly well suited both to building the conceptual bridges needed to initiate such an infusion of Buddhist thought into Chinese society and to articulate provisionally the meanings of the three "gates" or "entrances" of Buddhist practice. Zhuangzi's practical championing of "no-knowledge," "no-action," and "no-desire," for example, provided an apt Chinese cultural reference for deconstructing the samsara aspect of the three gates. No-knowledge meant refraining from fixed or principled discriminations, not holding onto any knowledge as absolute, and embracing the fluid relationships obtaining among all things. It accorded very well with the Mahayana Buddhist understanding of ignorance as a chronic failure to perceive the emptiness and interdependence of all things. No-action meant nonassertive, nonhabitual conduct and paralleled the Buddhist critique of habit formations.

Finally, no-desire—a capacity for leaving things as they are and craving nothing—was easily adopted as a referent for pivoting the Buddhist gate of clinging desire.

In general, Confucian thought and practice fared less well in setting up the foundations for Buddhist accommodation in China. But the central Confucian virtues of learning, personally demonstrating authoritative conduct, and cultivating ritual propriety were acceptable points of reference for qualifying the nirvana aspect of the three gates: wisdom, attentive virtuosity, and moral clarity. Moreover, there was significant sympathy between the Mahayana Buddhist aim of liberating all beings from suffering and the Mencian arguments for the inherent goodness of human nature. Indeed, Mencius' conviction that all people have the innate capacity for personal self-cultivation would later provide a native context for articulating one of Chinese Buddhism's most distinctive features—the teaching that all beings have buddha-nature.

Throughout the early phases of Buddhist accommodation in China, such parallels between Buddhist thought and China's indigenous traditions were actively sought and developed. Daoist terminology was widely used in translating Indian Buddhist concepts. For example, "*dao*" was variously used to render into Chinese the Indian words for the Buddhist path, spiritual discipline, and the Dharma, or teachings of the Buddha. At the same time, Buddhist texts that touched on such Confucian themes as respectful devotion to one's parents and the merits of benevolent government were actively circulated.

In some cases, considerable "interpretation" was needed to bring Buddhist and Chinese traditions into parallel. For example, while the celibacy required of Buddhist monks and nuns was often cited by Confucian critics as a violation of familial duty, Buddhist apologists argued that becoming an ordained monastic was even more meritorious and filial than having children. Buddhist narratives of ongoing life-to-life cycles often centered on the role of merit-making in changing one's karma and life story. As understood by the Chinese, however, individual life stories cannot be understood apart from those of families. In fact, the term used to translate "karma" into Chinese (*ye*) literally refers to one's entire personal and communal estate—one's entire life circumstances, centered on the family, and the opportunities they afford or inhibit. These understandings account for the popularity of stories in the *Lotus Sutra*—one of the most widely respected and revered Buddhist texts in China—that apparently depicted merit-making as a family affair affecting not only one's living relatives, but (at least potentially) one's ancestors as well.

Perhaps as important as the content of Buddhist texts, the strong association in China of writing and spiritual authority played a crucial role in the phase of accommodation. Writing had been intimately associated with authority in China since the Shang dynasty (roughly 1800 to 1100 B.C.E.), when it formed the basis of communication between the spirit realm and the ruling elite. By the time Buddhism began entering China in the Han dynasty, Chinese elite culture was profoundly literate. Texts—including historical, philosophical, and poetic works—not only served in the administration of governmental authority, they were vehicles for imagining the meaning of Chinese empire. By the late Zhou and Warring States periods, a relatively small body of texts like the *Yijing* had come to serve as sources of both inspiration and evaluation for scholar-officials crafting competing models of authority. Written texts thus functioned as shared foundations for intellectual society and (for certain special works) as objects with sacred status and virtually magical potency. The fact that Buddhism was a tradition that rested on a complex textual canon gave it significant authority—much more than a strictly ritualistic or purely meditative tradition would have commanded. The mutual accommodation of Buddhism and Chinese culture thus depended heavily on matching meanings across Confucian, Daoist, and Indian Buddhist texts.

At the same time, the gradual arrival of dozens and then hundreds of Buddhist texts gave shocking evidence of a literary galaxy that rivaled China's and, for the first time, forced it to become aware of its own limits. On one hand, the huge corpus of Buddhist texts translated into Chinese stimulated intense fascination. They revealed a radically alternative cosmos that was at once familiar enough to escape immediate rejection and novel enough to generate great intellectual and spiritual excitement. A contemporary parallel might be the publication of a previously unknown body of work giving evidence of a mature and fully systematic alternative to present Western scientific or medical traditions—an alternative that not only covers practically the same ground as ours, but reaches out into realms we had not even imagined possible. On the other hand, given the association of writing and authority in China, the growing body of Buddhist texts would have been viewed as both profoundly challenging and seductive. Anything that effectively threatened the status quo was, after all, also an alternative means of gaining, consolidating, and maintaining power—be it political, social, or religious.

Not surprisingly, international translation projects—often involving dozens of scholars—were sponsored by the imperial court and by wealthy members of society at large. As the Chinese Buddhist canon grew in size, however, so did concerns about how the body of Buddhist teachings was "originally" shaped. Which texts should be considered more basic and which seen as most spiritually advanced? In cases where texts contradicted each other—and in the absence of any reliable historical or cultural contexts for explaining such differences—how could they be reconciled systematically?

Texts had not entered China in any organized fashion. The literature of both Mahayana and Theravada traditions came over the Silk Road from Central Asia and India, none with dates of composition or any explicit hierarchic order. Buddhist texts in India—especially in the Theravada canon—were often collected according to such relatively arbitrary categories as total length or narrative themes and styles. Mahayana sutras were often set in patently ahistorical spaces and featured beings from a vast array of nonhuman realms.

By the seventh century, Buddhism had been in existence for one thousand years, and each of its diverse traditions had its own collection of core sutras (texts said to record the words of the Buddha) and sastras (commentaries by specialist Buddhist scholars). In the Buddhist universities of Central and South Asia—including at least one, Nalanda, with as many as ten thousand students and two thousand faculty in residence—these texts and commentaries formed basic curricula, and identifying and critically assessing differences among them was required. But the texts and commentaries randomly transmitted into China by traveling monks and merchants were part of no organized curriculum. It fell to Chinese Buddhists to decide how they should be ordered.

Chinese Buddhists naturally turned to the authority of the sutra literature that was held to record the words of the Buddha himself. New sutras were actively sought in the hope of clarifying the overall structure of the Dharma—the full body of teachings delivered by the Buddha. Each previously unknown sutra was greeted with expectations that it would allow all the others to fall into proper place and provide at least a glimpse of the Dharma as a whole. The excitement —both spiritual and intellectual—that each text would have generated can be imagined as comparable to the discovery of missing gospels recording the words of Jesus or lost books of the Hebrew scriptures.

Because many Mahayana sutras explicitly represented the Buddha as adjusting the content of his teachings in accordance with the needs of specific audiences, greater attention was eventually given to these texts and understanding their relationship to one another. Based partly on internal textual evidence and partly on Chinese cultural dispositions, several sutras emerged as centrally important. For example, the *Vimalakirti Sutra* depicted a lay student of the Buddha whose wisdom, attentive virtuosity, and moral clarity far exceeded those of all the (fully ordained) disciples who figured in the earliest sutra literature. Vimalakirti's lay status appealed to the Chinese not only because he represented a fully secular Buddhist ideal, but also because his spiritual attainments and insight were manifest throughout his daily affairs. His skill as a bodhisattva did not depend on demonstrated erudition or literary knowledge but on silent and unparalleled force of character. In the emergence of Chan, Vimalakirti's demonstration— not explanation—of the opening of the three gates of liberation would be taken as fully authoritative.

Other texts—most notably, the *Lotus, Flower Ornament,* and *Pure Land* sutras—offered such uniquely powerful visions of the cosmos that distinct schools formed around them. Often, the primary activity of these schools was scholastic—the work of translating and writing commentaries on its key texts. Up until the Song dynasty (tenth century c.e.), most monasteries would have groups of monks associated with each of these schools in residence. In the daily life of the monastic community, all monks—regardless of the school for which they felt the deepest affinity—would join in the performance of common rituals, undertake similar basic training in Buddhist mindfulness and calming, and follow the same monastic code. Because of their shared roots, these schools were often seen as separate branches of the buddha-dharma that traced their authority back through distinct textual genealogies—as individual families within the larger family of Buddhism.

In their search for the ultimate structure of the Dharma, Chinese Buddhist scholars mirrored their inherited cultural values of hierarchy and genealogy and eventually set about ranking Buddhist scriptures. Each school typically maintained that its core text was either first and foremost or historically most appropriate. Although new and revised rankings of Buddhist teachings would continue to be undertaken through at least the ninth century, the translation projects fueling them reached a turning point in the mid–seventh century with the work of the monk Xuanzang. From this point, Chinese Buddhists effectively turned their backs on Indian Buddhist textual traditions and struck out essentially on their own.

One can only speculate about the reasons for this abrupt loss of interest, especially in Indian commentarial texts, but it seems plausibly related to the controversies that embroiled Xuanzang on his return from sixteen years traveling in Central Asia and India. Although he returned to a hero's welcome and enjoyed great favor with the court, Xuanzang nevertheless came into significant conflict with fellow Chinese Buddhists on an issue that recalled the debate between Mencius and his opponents about the original goodness of human nature. Contrary to the dispositions of the vast majority of Chinese Buddhists, Xuanzang returned from India maintaining that there are people with such heavy karma that it is impossible for them ever to attain liberation. This "foreign" view was so troubling to the prevailing sensibilities of Chinese Buddhists that it was considered either to verge on the heretical or to require being understood as a perhaps conventionally useful but ultimately false teaching.

Although his journey was immortalized in the epic novel cycle *Journey to the West* (and these highly fictionalized adventures have fired China's imagination ever since), Xuanzang's Buddhist legacy was remarkably short-lived. His school dissolved within a few generations after his death, and Chinese Buddhism never again seriously considered the possibility that some beings are incapable of liberation. Text-

gathering missions to India ceased. Fully Chinese schools of Buddhism with their own authoritative commentarial traditions flourished. And, most important for the eventual emergence of Chan, the
genealogy of Buddhist thought and practice gradually became disen-
gaged from the transmission and translation of texts. Instead, it came
to be wedded to interpersonal lines of transmission—a shift from texts
to teachings understood as liberating relationships between teachers
and students.

Adaptation and Authority: The Phase of Advocacy

In addition to written texts and teachings, from very early on, meditation adepts with heightened perceptual capabilities and/or skills in
healing played a significant role in Buddhism's spread throughout
China. Such adepts were often invited to participate in government
and court rites, and occasionally to serve as official advisors. For the
vast, nonliterate rural population, the relative importance of such
adepts was even higher than in elite urban society. In responding to the
physical, emotional, and spiritual needs of villagers, meditation masters were able to introduce basic Buddhist concepts about suffering,
its causes, and its resolution. But in the context of such informal interactions—so very different from the highly choreographed conduct
required in elite circles—they were also in the position of actively
demonstrating the freely compassionate spirit of Buddhist practice.

The disparate significance of spiritual adepts and authoritative
texts in the countryside and urban society would come to play a major
role in the shift from Chinese Buddhist accommodation to advocacy.
It would also inform Chan's rise to almost unchallenged prominence
among the Chinese Buddhist schools by the second half of the ninth
century. Because the heavily text-centered schools of Chinese Buddhism—the Huayan *(Flower Ornament Sutra)* and Tiantai *(Lotus
Sutra)*—constructed their authority in ways familiar to the mainstream Chinese elite and were dependent on significant support from
the imperial court and the urban aristocracy, they were very vulnera-
ble to changes in political and economic climate. As a self-proclaimed
meditation school that eventually distanced itself from the imperial
court and was widely distributed in rural monasteries—especially in
regions far from the capital and China's political and economic cen-

ters—Chan was well positioned to survive both the indirect consequences of political upheaval and the much more direct effects of lost political and elite favor. Perhaps more important, the tensions between spiritual virtuosity and scholarly brilliance would be incorporated into Chan accounts of its own identity. Chan portrayed itself as a refreshingly rustic countercultural tradition committed not to the transmission of textual traditions from India, but to the flourishing of fully homegrown buddhas on native soil—enlightened Chinese masters whose teachings and social virtuosity outstripped those fostered by Confucianism and Daoism.

At the center of the controversy brought to a head by Xuanzang were the concepts of karma and buddha-nature. And, indeed, it is these two concepts that predominated in the Buddhist advocacy of a Chinese Middle Path that went between and well beyond both Confucian humanism and Daoist naturalism. In contrast with the concepts of change, interdependence, and emptiness, there were no indigenous Chinese analogues—even distant ones—for karma. Confucians and Daoists alike assumed a cosmological scheme derived from the *Yijing* in which change was constant, patterned, and inherently qualitative. It was not a view of change, however, in which intention was considered fundamental. From the perspective of the Buddhist teaching of karma, Confucianism and Daoism failed to take fully into account the irreducibly dramatic or meaningful nature of the cosmos. To generate practical insight into the interdependent arising and resolution of suffering, the roots of human temporality must be seen as value and intention.

The Confucian tradition focused primarily on renewing history through personal self-cultivation. Ending suffering involved (at the very least) insuring cultural continuity. This entailed both carefully rehearsing ritually inscribed memories and cultivating a capacity for reauthoring past precedents in present circumstances. The Daoist tradition focused on restoring the natural present by freeing it from encumbering cultural and personal overlays. Ending suffering took place through spontaneous transformations made possible when the human-scaled microcosm was harmonized with the cosmic Dao.

Mahayana Buddhism subverts the Confucian-Daoist polarity by suggesting that neither the past nor the present alone should occupy

full center stage but all three times: past, present, and future. The bodhisattva ideal involves understanding the historical precedents of
the present moment but not being bound by reliance upon them. It
involves skill in spontaneously removing relational blockages but not
becoming attached to the aim of free and easy wandering in the present. A Buddhist path toward resolving suffering involves dramatically revising the direction in which the interdependence of all things
is moving—a path of creatively engaging the future.

In an irreducibly karmic cosmos, there is no question of whether
things have a meaning or not but only of which meaning. It is a cosmos in which differences truly make a difference, in which changes of
heart are practically effective in reconfiguring the interpersonal present and future, and in which things are never just changing but always
going forward or going back. The teaching of karma urges human
beings to consider as crucial the direction of our life stories and the
values and intentions that establish it. Ultimately we are responsible
for whether we find the gates of our interdependence with all things
swinging in the direction of samsara or nirvana.

The karmic understanding of human temporality introduced the
Chinese to a new set of future-directed concerns. But it also under-
mined the primacy of a literal understanding of genealogy. Before the
Buddhist advocacy of a karmic understanding of change, the fabric of
Chinese society had been held together by ancestral lineages. The ritual structure of care was an effectively narrow one in which parents
faced the past to attend to their ancestors just as, one day, their own
children would attend to them. Although parents did have responsibility for raising their children and for carrying on the family line, the
sense of familial future was largely matter of fact, not dramatic. Seeing things karmically shifted the focus from attending to the past to
explicitly caring for future generations to a degree not found in Confucianism.

It also shifted the focus of care from literal ancestors and descen-
dents to partners related by shared values and intentions. Traditionally, one did not make offerings to the ancestors of neighbors or of
people from other villages. Concern for ancestral welfare was directed
along each family's blood lineage. The teaching of karma decentered
the notion of blood relations or genetic continuity. It pointed instead

toward the centrality of "dramatic continuity"—that is, continuity based on unwavering commitment to a particular direction for the meaning of things. This teaching radically altered the meaning of family.

In the *Lotus Sutra* and in the *Jataka Tales,* depicting the Buddha's prior lives, there are accounts of ensembles of characters—"dharma families"—moving together through time toward the shared realization of horizonless liberation. On these narrative journeys, members of the ensemble alternately play such dramatic roles as father, mother, son, daughter, king, minister, teacher, student, or friend. In contrast to the strict hierarchy of the Confucian family, the organization of such dharma families is not a function of birth order but of dramatic clarity. The dramatic ensemble centered on the historical Buddha included his wife and son, his parents, and each of his key disciples. It was deeply significant for Chinese Buddhists that the karma shared by each of these characters in the Buddha's life was so great that all attained liberation: freedom from suffering is not something realized alone or only for oneself.

Finally, the teaching of karma erases the horizons of responsibility that are part of our typical self-definition. Our presence together with others—our sharing of a particular world and history—is already evidence that we meaningfully belong together. We are not present together by accident. Neither are we present together because of some objective fate or destiny that transcends our personal sense of the meaning of things. The first step in resolving the conflicts so characteristic of our shared lives is neither the Confucian one of establishing binding cultural precedents and principles, nor the Daoist one of reverting to intention-free naturalness. Rather, it is realizing the absence of any absolute boundaries separating us from our situations and the possibility of completely revising their meaning. Doing so, we can truly accord with our situation and respond as needed to direct it away from samsara toward nirvana. But realizing this absence of boundaries is also seeing that we cannot truly save any one being without saving all beings. The teaching of karma, understood in this way, reveals the bodhisattva vow of liberating all sentient beings as the root condition for realizing any liberation at all.

The second central concept in the advocacy of Chinese Buddhism is that of buddha-nature. Although it is loosely related to certain Indian teachings about the "womb or embryo of thusness" and the "treasury or storehouse consciousness," the concept of buddha-nature is distinctively Chinese. Many alternative accounts could be given for the rise of this concept in China and how it was incorporated into the theories and practices of the four major schools of Chinese Buddhism. Common to all such accounts, however, is recognizing that the concept of buddha-nature served to characterize positively the meaning of emptiness, to link the interdependence of all things with their interpenetration or mutual nonobstruction, and to insist on the possibility of liberation, here and now, for each and every one of us.

Buddha-nature thought is deeply rooted in Chinese conceptions of the dynamic and relational nature of all things. If all things are interdependent with all other things, and if the nature of all things is relational and dispositional, then the appearance of one buddha is the (at least potential) appearance of all buddhas. It is also the transformation of the entire world in which this appearance takes place. If all things are both interdependent and interpenetrating, then the presence of a buddha in this world realm is the presence of a buddha throughout this world realm. Thus, the Chan Buddhist master Hongren said that the ultimate practice of Chan is realizing that the true body of the Buddha and the nature of sentient beings are the same.

The point here is that the limitless positive and liberating qualities of a Buddha do not transcend our familiar world but are always and everywhere present within it. That is, movement in the direction of nirvana is part of the nature of all things. As it would come to be understood in Chan, Buddhist practice does not consist of a method for arriving at the end of liberation but a method for its actualization and demonstration.

The concept of buddha-nature thus performed the countercultural service of cutting through the opposition of Confucian self-cultivation (with its emphasis on clear and formal goals for exemplary conduct) and Daoist no-cultivation (with its emphasis on undirected spontaneity). From the perspective of Chinese Buddhists, both are mistaken. The culture-consolidating efforts recommended by Confucianism err in establishing a bias toward fixed standards and the inculcation of habit formations. They mean an intensifying karma for suffering, because they involve ignoring the fluid interdependence of all things and the necessity of improvisational skill and creativity in responding to situational needs. Likewise, the culture-subverting effortlessness recommended by Daoism errs in celebrating a failure to address the present situation critically. Simply following what comes naturally means acting on the basis of previously conditioned patterns of ignorance and thus failing to revise one's karma and the meaning of things.

By contrast, Buddhist practice focuses on giving situationally and critically responsive form to the emptiness or interdependence of all things. As such, it means both fully appreciating our circumstances and skillfully contributing to their expression of a truly liberating intimacy among all things. Buddhist practice does not bring about the resolution of suffering by establishing an utterly secure place in the world for the practitioner or by a retreat to "no-place" in the world. It does so by opening for revision the meaning of our entire world as the true buddha-body.

The First Schools of Chinese Buddhism

Buddhist advocacy in China came to fruition in the sixth to ninth centuries with the consolidation of four major schools of Chinese Buddhism: Tiantai, Huayan, Pure Land, and Chan. All mounted explicit critiques of China's native traditions of Confucianism and Daoism and provided what they argued were more complete and effective methods for addressing the problem of suffering and realizing true freedom. Of these, only Pure Land and Chan would survive the persecutions of 842–845 as distinct, ongoing traditions.

TIANTAI (HEAVENLY TERRACE)

The Tiantai tradition derived its name from the sacred mountain in Zhejiang province where its central monastic center was located. Founded by the monk Huisi (515–576), Tiantai was given its most extensive and influential expression in the work of his immediate dharma heir, Zhiyi (538–597). Indeed, as far as Chinese in the sixth and seventh centuries were concerned, Zhiyi's writings settled once and for all any questions about textual inconsistencies in the Buddhist canon. His classification of Buddhist texts not only made their consistent organization possible, it also accommodated and accorded well with important strands of native Chinese thought on the relationship between language and truth.

Zhiyi took as his hermeneutical starting point the Mahayana teaching of the emptiness of all things. If all things are absent any inherent and essential nature, then no verbal formulation of the truth can be seen as final, since all words refer to conceptually identifiable phenomena. At best, they can point through phenomena toward underlying patterns of relationship or governing principles. They cannot provide direct access. Indeed, Zhiyi maintained that any verbal statement can only be partially true. The most comprehensive—and thus most true—statements are not those that exclude all others, but rather those that embrace contradiction and plurality. For Zhiyi, no Buddhist teaching so thoroughly expressed this truth than the teaching that all beings have buddha-nature or the nature of enlightenment. And, in his estimation, no Buddhist text more profoundly revealed this truth than the *Lotus Sutra*. Zhiyi was also responsible for writing the single most influential meditation manual in Chinese Buddhist history (one on which many Chan teachers would draw): *The Great Calm Abiding and Insight Meditation.*

Tiantai teachings appealed greatly to members of the Sui court, and the school received significant royal patronage. This worked against the tradition, however, when the Sui fell. Although still an important tradition, Tiantai lost a certain degree of its prestige and prominence.

HUAYAN (FLOWER ORNAMENT)

The Huayan tradition considers its first patriarch to have been a famed meditative adept and healer named Dushun (557–640), but the first extant references to a distinctive Huayan school occurred only in the latter part of the seventh century in association with Fazang (643–712), traditionally the third Huayan lineage holder. Along with the fifth patriarch Zongmi (780–841)—who had the distinction of also being a Chan lineage holder—Fazang was considered the primary architect of Huayan Buddhism.

Like Zhiyi, Fazang was a firm believer in the teaching of buddha-nature and the interdependence and interpenetration of all things. Unlike his Tiantai counterpart, however, he did not believe that the "one (or unifying) vehicle" taught by the *Lotus Sutra* marked the most complete and sophisticated expression of the Buddha's Dharma. Much of his lifework consisted of explicating the meaning of the *Avatamsaka Sutra,* or *Huayan Sutra*—a text that in English translation runs well over 1,500 pages in length and that is surely among the most baroquely detailed descriptions of extraordinary awareness in world literature.

The key to Fazang's reading of the *Huayan Sutra* is his commitment to seeing buddha-nature—and thus the root or original nature of all things—as impartially and clearly reflecting the contributions of all things to their shared situation. That is, the true nature of things is to reflect or confirm the contributions of all other things. His famous image of this idea was the metaphor of Indra's net—a space in which each and every point is a mirror reflecting the reflections within all other mirrors (including itself) to infinity. Because mutuality is the very nature of things, not only do causes condition their effects, effects also condition their causes. Indeed, it can be said that all things are identical precisely in the sense that all things are always reflecting and thus contributing to their shared situation all that has come to be thus, in this particular way. Buddhist enlightenment was not, for Fazang, an escape from phenomenal reality but its clear and compassion embrace.

If Tiantai provided the seminal Chinese description of meditation, Huayan provided the quintessential Chinese expression of the Buddhist worldview. Both traditions, however, were heavily text-focused. With the purge of Buddhism in the mid–ninth century, the libraries and scholarly circles that constituted the life-blood of Tiantai and Huayan were destroyed. It was not until the eleventh century, when Korean monks began to bring Tiantai and Huayan texts back into China, that the traditions started to reform. But by this time, Pure Land and Chan were firmly established as the central axes of popular and elite Chinese Buddhist practice and society.

QINGTU (PURE LAND)

The Qingtu or Pure Land tradition was founded in the early sixth century by a northerner named Tanluan (476–542), who was first introduced to Buddhism sometime after the arrival of the Indian Buddhist meditation master Bodhiruci in Luoyang in 508 C.E. Using the

Sukhavati-vyuha Sutra as a textual locus for his teaching, Bodhiruci informed Tanluan that he was not likely to have time in this life to overcome his karmic blockages and realize full Buddhist awakening. But, if he sincerely and constantly practiced the recitation of the Buddha Amitabha's name, he would be granted birth in that buddha's Western Paradise or Pure Land. Indeed, the Buddha Amitabha had vowed to answer the appeals of suffering beings in all realms and at all times, insuring their birth in circumstances in which enlightenment was practically guaranteed.

In keeping with the general trend of Chinese Buddhism, Tanluan interpreted the *Sukhavati-vyuha Sutra* in light of the then developing Chinese conception of buddha-nature. In his teaching of Pure Land Buddhism, he thus stressed the universal possibility of awakening for all beings, without exception, if they were simply to place their faith in Amitabha and his vow. But unlike the nascent Tiantai and Huayan traditions, Tanluan did not offer much hope of receiving rewards of any sort in this life by practicing Buddhism. The point of reciting the Buddha's name was not to awaken here and now, but rather to insure birth in circumstances that would guarantee full awakening.

At first, Pure Land teachings appealed to China's socially and politically disenfranchised: commoners, merchants, and members of non-Han Chinese ethnic groups. But after the An Lushan rebellion and the decade of horror following it, the tradition found considerable appeal in the court and elite social circles as well. The emphasis on continuous practice, in any situation whatsoever, was taken up by the Chan traditions in the eighth and ninth centuries and found common ground in the Huayan practice of group sutra recitations. Eventually, the use of chanting and recitation became a common heritage of Chinese Buddhist practice. Indeed, it was possible for Zongmi to state without any controversy that Chan mindfulness and Pure Land recitation were just two sides of a single process of realizing our original buddha-nature. Although most Chan teachers would follow the sixth Chan patriarch, Huineng, in declaring that the Pure Land is not some other realm but our own pure and clear mind in this very moment, all were comfortable embracing the consonance of Pure Land practice with Chan.

Over time, the importance of Pure Land as an independent school waned. Its core practices and teachings were functionally absorbed as skillful means into the practice traditions of Huayan, Tiantai, and Chan. As such Pure Land practices continue to be a part of the Chinese Buddhist experience to this day, especially in village settings.

From Orthodoxy to Orthopraxy:
The Crucial Tide Change in Chinese Buddhism

The concepts of karma and buddha-nature played an undeniably crucial role in the advocacy of Buddhism in China. But they also proved crucial in bringing about a crisis in the search for Buddhist orthodoxy —a crisis out of which Chan would eventually emerge as a preeminent form of Chinese Buddhism. A central theme found in each of the Mahayana texts about which the first Chinese schools of Buddhism coalesced was *upaya,* or skillful means. Perhaps most explicitly and thoroughly expressed in the *Lotus Sutra,* skillful means referred to the creative devices employed by bodhisattvas in carrying out their vow to liberate all sentient beings. Great bodhisattvas possessed such profound skill in means that there were no situations in which they could not do the buddha-work of awakening. That is, they were able to attune their way of relating and teaching so precisely to the needs of their audiences that none could remain turned toward samsara rather than nirvana.

The Buddha crafted his teachings to meet the particular and differing needs of his various Indian audiences. Indeed, in many Mahayana sutras and throughout the commentarial tradition, contradictions in the teachings were explained by specific reference to the Buddha's exercise of skillful means. But what, then, could be said of the needs of Chinese audiences? If Chinese audiences differed from those living a thousand years earlier in India, what relevance would an orthodoxy founded on Indian texts have for a Chinese audience? Much as it had been necessary for the Buddha to improvise new vocabularies and rhetorical strategies in the course of his teaching career, would it not be necessary for Buddhists to do the same in China? And, if it was true that all beings are capable of expressing buddha-nature, what could possibly stand in the way of this being done by Chinese Buddhists?

Granted the literary bias of Chinese elite culture and the role of written texts in establishing and maintaining authority, the first overtures in this direction came in the form of Chinese compositions of new Buddhist sutras—that is, texts purporting to transmit the teachings of the historical Buddha himself. An influential example is the *Sutra of Perfect Enlightenment.* Also crucial were Chinese-composed treatises that represented themselves as the work of eminent Indian commentators. The most widely disseminated and respected of these is the *Awakening of Mahayana Faith,* a seminal sixth-century text that helped shape the curriculum of all Chinese schools of Buddhism and that expressed the inseparability of faith or confidence and practice or actualizing enlightenment.

In many ways, the composition of apocryphal texts can be seen as a bridge between the accommodations that had centered on translating Indian and Central Asian texts into Chinese and the unabashed advocacy of Buddhism for and by Chinese. In addition to their insightful expressions of Buddhist teachings in ways suited to Chinese audiences, such apocryphal texts evidence an unwillingness fully to own these as Chinese Buddhist teachings. Finally, their authority is not based on force of character—confidence in their own expressive quality—but on their attribution to luminous foreign buddhas and Buddhists.

Buddhist apocrypha in China arose out of a crisis regarding the appropriateness of transmitted forms of Buddhist orthodoxy and growing self-confidence about being able to close the gap of authority between Indian and Chinese Buddhists. But they did not yet engage Chinese audiences in living demonstrations of how buddha-nature is restored and revealed. Even if their questionable provenance was allowed to pass unnoticed, it remained true that they did not record live responses made to explicitly and concretely Chinese questions, concerns, and conflicts. They were, at best, generic responses to the needs of Chinese audiences. As skillful means, Buddhist apocrypha were not fully mature.

The functional inadequacy of such texts went, however, much deeper. In marked contrast with the situation prevailing in Indian cultural spheres, the doctrinal authority of a written text in China was not inherent to the text itself. That is, authoritative texts were not assumed to be analytically self-validating. Instead, they were taken as publicly validated—if at all—in the ways that familiarity with them characteristically transformed human conduct. In other words, knowledge does not refer to true states of belief; it means knowing how and not just knowing that. Finally, written teachings or doctrines are just distillations of practice. Chinese cultural convictions about the efficacy of writing and about the embodied nature of knowledge thus entailed treating any crisis in orthodoxy as essentially a crisis in orthopraxy.

The composition of apocryphal texts could not be a substitute for the Chinese Buddhist demonstration of skillful means—the practice of exemplary, bodhisattva conduct. Furthermore, since the major doctrinal innovation in these texts centered on the concept of buddhanature, this demonstration would necessarily have to be utterly exemplary—nothing short of the manifestation of a "homegrown" buddha. Not surprisingly, the crisis in Buddhist orthodoxy marked a shift of attention away from scholarly Buddhist circles—the masters of words and letters—toward the spiritual mastery of Buddhist meditative adepts. Chinese Buddhism could not, finally, rest solely (or even mainly) on texts composed in China by and for Chinese. If it was to grow at all, it had to grow out of a demonstrated ability to enter liberating forms of interdependence—to swing the gate of ignorance open onto wisdom, the gate of habit formations onto attentive virtuosity, and the gate of clinging desire onto moral clarity. This was the founding work and perennial legacy of Chan.

CHAPTER 4

The Early History of the Chan Tradition

In sharp contrast with the three other major schools of Chinese Buddhism, Chan did not originate in the Chinese appropriation of Indian Buddhist texts. Instead, its origins can be traced to the appropriation of Indian Buddhist practices—their adoption by and adaptation to the needs of Chinese Buddhists. As it would come to describe itself by at least the late tenth century, Chan developed as a "practice lineage," not a doctrinal school. As encapsulated in slogans repeated throughout East Asia by the middle of the Song dynasty, Chan was a "special transmission, beyond words and letters," that was based on "directly pointing toward the human mind, seeing one's nature, and becoming a Buddha."

As the fourth major way of Chinese Buddhism and the last to develop, Chan did not come about in a historical vacuum. It arose after half a millennium of accommodation between imported traditions of Buddhism and China's native cultural traditions. As conveyed through texts brought from India and Central Asia, Buddhist teachings had already taken deep root in Chinese culture. To extend the agricultural metaphor, over the centuries that Indian Buddhist teachings were being seeded into Chinese culture and society, some (like those of the Mahayana) proved readily compatible with the local climate while others did not. According to the metaphor, the great text-focused schools of Chinese Buddhism—Tiantai, Huayan, and Pure Land—derived from individual seed stocks that produced great and enduring groves of unified textual and ritual tradition. Chan was very different.

According to the best contemporary scholarship, Chan did not develop out of any single doctrinal tradition or in any single original locale. Although tradition traces the initial flowering of Chan to the late-fifth-century arrival in China of the south Indian meditation master Bodhidharma, there is little evidence of a coherent Chan genealogy much before the eighth century. Instead, the seeds from which Chan developed were not all of a single type, and each strain underwent significant and largely independent adaptation in China's cultural soil. Simply stated, the historical record strongly suggests that Chan was quilted or grafted together over a period of two or three centuries as a pluralistic system. It was not until the last decades of the Tang dynasty that a relatively stable genealogy was firmly in place and not until the early Song that Chan was routinely summarized as a special transmission outside the teachings, not depending on words and letters, pointing directly at the human mind and becoming a Buddha. Incorporating many different strains of teaching and practice, Chan has all along been an ecological tradition—a highly diverse "dharma rainforest."

Of particular importance in reconstructing the early years of Chan have been texts and historical records that were most likely archived during the eighth and ninth centuries in the libraries of Tibet and at Dunhuang—an important city on the northern Silk Road in China. Most of these texts were recovered only at the turn of the last century, and many are only now being given serious attention. On the whole, they provide a glimpse of the Buddhist scene during the formative years of Chan that differs in some important respects from the description given in later Chan histories. Such texts describe a time of great spiritual creativity in which Chinese Buddhists found their own distinctive voices and accepted active responsibility for expressing their own original buddha-nature.

The traditional internal narrative of the birth of Chan begins decisively with the arrival of Bodhidharma and charts an unbroken lineage of direct transmissions of the Buddha's wisdom, attentive virtuosity, and moral clarity from one Chan generation to the next. The continuous thread in this lineage of "gate-opening" relationships between teachers and students consists of the unwavering presence of a unique spirit or relational vitality. And in traditional Chan accounts of its own origins, it is this spirit that is granted priority—the lived meaning of truly liberating intimacy and compassion.

If the historical account of Chan's origins effectively suppresses

Chan's spiritual brilliance, however, the traditional account arguably errs in stressing the uniqueness of Chan's commitment to practice as opposed to doctrine. All of the other major schools of Chinese Buddhism also had ongoing traditions of meditative discipline or attention training. All were committed to the innovative Chinese conception of buddha-nature and a positive reading of emptiness *(sunyata)* as horizonless interrelatedness. Moreover, although they were founded on the authority of originally Indian texts and teachings, all three grew through the interpretative medium of commentaries written by Chinese—often at significant odds with Indian commentarial traditions. The shared ground among all four Chinese Buddhist traditions is substantial.

All the same, Chan did come to differ in important ways from Tiantai, Huayan, and Pure Land—ways that were to insure its unbroken practice, in China, down to the present day. These differences can be highlighted maximally by looking at the meaning of meditation and the primacy of teaching as a dynamic relationship and by considering how these contributed to new, specifically Chan constructions of the gates of wisdom, attentive virtuosity, and moral clarity.

In Huayan, meditation and sutra recitation served as crucial supports for intellectual insight into the interdependence and interpenetration of all things. As such, they can be seen as resulting in the acknowledgment of the true and original nature of things—the attainment of wisdom. From a Chan perspective, such an understanding of wisdom is entirely too thin. Buddhist wisdom does not simply consist in seeing what buddha-nature is, but also means realizing in direct social demonstration what buddha-nature does. In this, Chan exemplifies a general Chinese disinterest in metaphysics and a correlative concern for relational transformation. Thus, Chan masters from Huineng onward invoked the inseparability of meditation and wisdom. Just as a body and its activity or functioning are only analytically distinct, meditation and wisdom are simply twin aspects of the nondual expression of buddha-nature or enlightening conduct.

Likewise, the very sophisticated description and practice of meditation in the Tiantai tradition was criticized as aiming only for complete and comprehensive awareness—that is, a capacity to embrace or include all things. While there is nothing inherently incorrect about this aim, it is not a sufficient corrective for human suffering. For Chan, meditation means the expression of attentive virtuosity. It is not enough simply to be able to perceive all things calmly and with insight. Indeed, there is a liability in pressing too far in the direction of simple equanimity: an absence of reasons to act with compassion on behalf of all sentient beings. Attentive virtuosity means being able to accord with each and every situation and respond as needed, whether it is a situation of utter complacency or utmost crisis.

Finally, Chan represents a reframing of moral clarity that emphasizes meaningful improvisation and not a simple adherence to rules and precedents. Although this emphasis left some Chan practitioners (especially in eighth-century Sichuan province) open to charges of antinomianism and amorality, its more widespread effect was to encourage cutting through the presuppositions about what is possible and what is impossible—presuppositions that severely constrain one's ability to carry out the bodhisattva work of shifting the movement within each situation away from samsara toward nirvana. On the one hand, this led to valorizing the "true person of no rank" who is freely able to contribute to any situation as needed, unbound by the constraints of societal rules and roles. On the other, it led Chan masters to denounce the aim of Pure Land practice even while acknowledging its efficacy in attention training. In the words of Huineng, "It is your own mind that is the Pure Land." Salvation is possible here and now, in this very life.

Unlike the other schools of Chinese Buddhism, Chan did not valorize learning about the Buddha Dharma or teachings transmitted from India and Central Asia. It did not expend any energy on trying to organize those teachings or establish a hierarchy among them. Instead, it insisted on the possibility of expressing, in any circumstances whatsoever, our true and original buddha-nature. This one learned to do through entering into close and unprecedented relationship with a skilled and truly enlightening master. Book learning was, if anything, likely to be an impediment. What was crucial was the opportunity to encounter a direct, spiritual descendant of the Buddha—a true lineage holder in an unbroken line of transmission. The possibility of Chan rested, in short, on the emergence in China of homegrown buddhas.

This insistence on the centrality of a lived relationship in the realization of Chan is summarized in the phrase "a special transmission, beyond words and letters." This translation obscures, however, the radically countercultural turn taken by Chan. The Chinese terms commonly translated as "words and letters"—*wen* and *zi*—have important connotations that are not captured in the English phrase and that clearly position Chan in a critical relationship with Chinese culture.

"Wen" originally referred to patterned regularities found both in nature and in human community. By extension, it came to refer broadly to culture and more specifically to the literary embodiment of cultural precedents. *"Zi"* is composed of the character for "child" under the "house" radical and originally meant to breed, nourish, bring up, or treat with fatherly love. It later came to mean a name, word, or written character. The connection here rests on the role of the written word in traditional Chinese understandings of self-cultivation and authority. As mentioned earlier, Chinese traditionally held that writing originated as the central medium of communication between the celestial and the human. It thus offered a means of regulating human conduct in keeping with the *dao* or patterning inherent to the cosmos as a whole. Learning to read and write meant duplicating, in and for oneself, the patterns of cultural precedent on which personal development and social and political harmony depended.

By positioning itself as a special transmission outside the teachings, not depending on words and letters, Chan claimed separation from the modes of authority fixed by Chinese tradition. Not depending on words and letters signaled Chan's willingness to criticize and transgress the cultural precedents and structures of mediation invoked by Chinese tradition. At the same time, however, it signaled a willingness among Chan practitioners to downplay the authority of text-based Buddhist teachings and to allow their own conduct to speak for itself.

This confidence led some Chan masters to go so far as to disparage Buddhist sutras and commentaries as "hitching posts for donkeys"—fixed points of reference for those incapable of appreciative and contributory virtuosity. Because this confidence emerged in the context of relational improvisations involving students and Chinese Buddhist teachers, it can be argued—as I have done elsewhere and at length (see Further Reading)—that Chan also came to differ markedly from other forms of Chinese Buddhism by clearly and emphatically situating enlightenment in relationship. Chan enlightenment was not realized as the experience of an individual but only in the situational expression of buddha-nature in the drama of day-to-day life. For Chan, enlightenment was not just a possibility for all beings but necessarily realized with them.

By shifting its claim to authority from written texts and teachings to living teachers and the relationships they realized in direct encounter with their disciples, Chan was able to situate itself fully within Chinese culture. This radical shift enabled Chan to undertake a countercultural advocacy of Buddhism that was both broad and deep. But it also opened the possibility of undertaking an important countercultural —and yet profoundly ethical, not metaphysical—critique of other dominant forms of Buddhism in China. As many of the materials recovered from Dunhuang make clear, in the very earliest forms of Chan there was already a frankly maverick sensibility. Chan was radical in the twin senses of advocating a personal and direct return to (what it described as) the true roots of Buddhism and advocating a creative rooting in the vernaculars and values of specifically Chinese culture.

For example, it is now clear that while the arrival of Bodhidharma in China was a watershed in the emergence of a distinctively Chan approach to Buddhism, his reception by Chinese Buddhists was not unilateral. In the circle of spiritual and meditative adepts that formed in northern China around Bodhidharma and his closest associates, there were two main camps. In the first were those who effectively followed the major Indian commentarial traditions in understanding his teachings and the purposes of meditation. For them, meditative discipline consisted of a gradual winnowing out of unclear thought patterns and finally realizing a state of calm abstraction from the turmoil of sensory experience—a course of increasingly refined awareness culminating in the experience of supranormal perceptual abilities and insights.

In the other camp, there were those like the little-known Master Yuan who understood Bodhidharma's teachings and practice style as a radical critique of precisely such views. For them, relying on scriptures and commentaries and hoping to clear the mind gradually to the point of achieving absolute peace are obstructions on the path. Asked by a student what is meant by the phrase "a demon mind," Master Yuan answered that a demon mind is sitting silently in a cross-legged position with your eyes closed and entering a state of supreme concentration. He even went so far as to suggest that having a "nonmoving mind"—one of the staple goals of traditional Indian sitting meditation—is just "bondage *samadhi.*"

For Master Yuan and those aligned with him, verbal teachings fared no better than step-by-step methods of meditation. Echoing the silence of Vimalakirti and presaging future generations of Chan Buddhist masters, Master Yuan insisted that he had no teaching to convey and that words and written texts are deceptions that can only stifle bodily energy and spirit and make it impossible truly to conduct oneself as a buddha. Ultimately, there can be no question of following rules or principles or gradual courses of study in expressing our buddha-nature and entering into enlightening relationships as bodhisattvas.

The strategic differences between these camps would play a continuing role in the transition from accommodation to advocacy as Chinese Buddhism matured in the sixth through ninth centuries. In particular, they would reflect different approaches to negotiating the proper balance among political, social, and spiritual concerns as China's long period of disunity came to an end and the imperial center once again strengthened. An important turning point early in this process was the purge of Buddhism ordered by Emperor Wu of the Zhou between 574 and 577. Monasteries and temples were destroyed, Buddhist libraries were burned, and several hundred thousand monks and nuns were returned to lay society or drafted into corvée labor. But in addition, Wu also ordered that a steering committee of Buddhist monks be constituted to lead a reformation of Buddhism in China. These monks were selected on the basis of espousing beliefs and standards of practice that resonated well with the needs of the court and established a clear basis for government oversight with respect to the internal dynamics of the Buddhist community.

At the time of the purge and its aftermath, many of those in the Bodhidharma circle either fled to the mountains or went "underground" in lay society. Arguably, much of the rhetoric leveled against the gradualist and text-fascinated camps by proto-Chan teachers like Master Yuan pivoted on the liability of its members for being coopted into the imperial demand for a well-behaved, tightly organized, and respectfully quietist Buddhist community. Indeed, the tension between these camps only resolved in the early to mid–eighth century, when Chan was forced to confront and reconcile differences in its strategic identity as an advocate of truly radical Buddhist practice. This occurred in the capital of Luoyang with the famous rift between the so-called northern and southern schools of Chan.

Toward the end of the seventh century, the East Mountain school in rural Hubei province emerged as the most prominent of the early Chan traditions, and its leader, Hongren, was widely identified as the fifth in a direct line of descent from Bodhidharma. At the turn of the eighth century, word of the school had spread to the court, and the Empress Wu invited one of Hongren's senior students, Shenxiu, to lecture in the palace. Shenxiu taught a blend of Tiantai meditation techniques and discourses on the "sudden and complete" teaching of buddha-nature, urging a gradual dissociation of our pure and original nature from the defilements of everyday human thoughts and awareness. His version of Chan sufficiently impressed the imperial court that he was invited to remain in the capital, established as an advisor to the court, and introduced to Luoyang's elite society. His school strengthened and would enjoy substantial patronage for several generations.

But in 730 trouble started. Shenxiu's claim to Chan authority came under public challenge from a monk named Shenhui who was teaching just south of the capital in Nanyang. Shenhui had studied briefly under Hongren and Shenxiu but claimed to have matured under the guidance of a second, little-known student of Hongren—the soon-to-be-famous Huineng. Shenhui charged that Shenxiu and his heirs had wrongly taken the patriarchal mantle in the lineage of Bodhidharma and Hongren, usurping the rightful place of Huineng, the legitimate sixth patriarch of Chan. It was Huineng, argued Shenhui, who had inherited the true sudden practice taught by Hongren and who had received as a symbol of this transmission Hongren's robe and bowl—the very robe passed down from generation to generation from the Buddha through Bodhidharma and on to Hongren. Shenxiu's teaching of meditative gradualism leading to an inward realization of unbroken equanimity was a false reading of Chan. Meditation was not an indwelling process of experiential release—a function of sitting still with eyes closed, concentrating on the breath or some other focus of attention. Meditation was wisdom in action.

All of these charges were levied in a public council convened by Shenhui for the purpose of purifying the tradition and restoring the roots of Chan. A complete record of this council and its exact outcome are no longer extant. It is clear, however, that the "northern school" of Chan did suffer a great loss of prestige and that Shenhui's genealogy of the "southern school" eventually became accepted by all of the Chan traditions surviving into the ninth century. Given the extant eighth-century literature on Shenhui, it is arguable that his advocacy of Hui-neng's approach to Chan was successful in its own terms, for reasons rooted in the historical context of Chinese culture and society. Shen-hui himself was viewed by many as overly ambitious, self-promoting, and given to spiteful and discordant campaigns against those who blocked his own advancement. Indeed, his own lineage was not partic-ularly long-lived and faded from view with the death of Zongmi—the last Chan lineage holder claiming descent from Huineng via Shenhui.

The tragic decade from 754 to 763 brought about a widespread col-lapse of all institutionalized forms of authority. With their legacy of rural practice, the early Chan traditions—especially those in central and southwest China, far from the imperial capital—were well situated to survive the waves of military, economic, and political chaos that swept the country. Out of this, there emerged a set of strong Chan traditions dedicated to the demonstration of responsive virtuosity. Among these, three were particularly vibrant.

The Niutou, or Oxhead, school, claiming a separate lineage back to the fourth Chan patriarch, Daoxin, and the likely point of origin for the *Platform Sutra* of Huineng, would fade from view by the end of the ninth century. But the traditions established in the eighth century by two of Huineng's "grandsons" in the Dharma would spawn the so-called Five Houses of Chan and have survived to the present day. To Chan master Shitou can be traced the houses or family lines of Cao-dong, Fayan, and Yunmen Chan. Out of Chan master Mazu's Hong-zhou school—spread throughout Jiangxi and Hubei provinces and centered on his distinctive use of "shock tactics" and the absence of any barriers between awakening and ordinary mind—there emerged the houses of Guiyang and Linji.

As the Tang dynasty began crumbling in the late ninth century and China fell into another period of disunity, internal tensions with Chan's identity came again to the foreground. While the lineages from Huineng through Mazu had survived the persecutions of Buddhism in 845, and Linji Chan (later known in Japan as Rinzai Zen) and Cao-dong Chan (later, Soto Zen) were emerging as the most vibrant traditions of Chinese Buddhism, there was great political pressure for Buddhism to play a moderating or reconciliatory role nationwide. Within Chan, the crucial question was whether Chan transmission took place in accord with the teachings and the fixed institutional structures these implied or if it took place "outside the teachings."

The followers of Linji during the Five Dynasties period between the Tang and the Song were adamant that Chan retain its critical role—not only with respect to Buddhist structures of authority but vis-à-vis Confucianism and Daoism as well. Others advocated a "harmony between Chan and the teachings" and promoted Buddhism as a force for reconciliation and the restoration of social and political stability. Most notable among the latter group were the followers of Fayan (885–958) located in the small but culturally and economically important kingdoms of Jiangxi and Wuyue. Wedded as it was to the long-standing Chinese concern for cultural continuity and stability, so-called Wuyue Buddhism was very appealing to those seeking the political reunification of China. In addition, several of the more prominent teachers associated with the movement urged syntheses between Chan and other forms of Chinese Buddhism as well as respect for many Confucian and Daoist values. This drive toward functional syncretism came to be a lasting factor in the popular practice of religion in China and the belief that, at root, "the three teachings are one."

Linji's radical Chan rejected not only Indian texts and teachings but the Chinese classics as "hitching posts for donkeys." It also promoted a deep celebration of the dramatic correctives that emerged in the context of student encounters with indigenous or homegrown buddhas. In combination, these made it imperative that advocates of critical Chan craft a self-consistent, legitimating narrative capable of warranting its right to express and establish the full meaning of Buddhist practice and awakening. At the center of this narrative—around which there consolidated a lasting and exclusively Chan sense of Buddhist identity—was an (apparently apocryphal) exchange between the Buddha and his disciple Mahakasyapa.

Shenhui had already argued that Huineng was the legitimate heir of Bodhidharma's teaching and practice by citing Hongren's hand-to-hand transmission to him of the Buddha's robe and bowl. According to Shenhui, this was the thirty-third in series of such transmissions beginning with the Buddha's gift of these items to Mahakasyapa. By at least the beginning of the eleventh century, the exact nature of this original transmission came into rhetorical focus.

For example, in the *Gateless Frontier Pass (Wumen guan)*, this exchange is directly presented as the seminal "transmission outside the teachings"—the original instance of enlightening, silent resonance between Buddhist teacher and Buddhist student. Asked to teach before a large assembly on Vulture Peak, the Buddha is said to have simply held up a single flower. So unexpected was this response that the entire assembly was left speechless. Only Mahakasyapa understood the Buddha's action and broke into a smile. The Buddha then stated that he held the treasury of the true dharma eye, the wondrous mind of nirvana, the handle on the formless dharma gate of the formlessness of true form—a dharma not depending on words and letters, a special transmission outside the teachings. "This," he said, "I offer to Mahakasyapa."

Why did Chan advocates single out Mahakasyapa as their ancestral link to the Buddha? No internal Chan discussion of this is extant. Nor would one be expected, given Chan's expressed affirmation of this exchange and the spiritual genealogy resulting from it as simple historical realities. It is interesting, though, to note that Mahakasyapa's first instructions from the Buddha involved cultivating a sense of shame about prior wrongdoings, respecting the lineage of his teachers, and practicing continuous mindfulness of the body combined with gladness. These elements became important parts of Chan's practical structure. Shame also plays a powerful role in the Confucian construction of self-cultivation. For Chinese audiences, its social function would have been apparent. But from a Buddhist perspective, there is a subversive element in shame: it is not something objectively imposed by external authorities, but rather a recognition, in oneself, of the quality of one's conduct. To cultivate a sense of shame is to become fully responsible for oneself, to hold within oneself the power of authoring virtuosity. This idea accorded rather well with Chan's critical stance and its conviction that it is possible—here and now— to become a buddha.

Importantly, Mahakasyapa was also renowned for his ability to associate freely with laypeople, taking joy in their joys, finding Buddhist fortunes in their good fortune, and demonstrating the meaning of awakening in even the most mundane circumstances. This relational skill was said to be a function of his deep capacity for attentive virtuosity, or *samadhi*. Like the Mahayana figure Vimalakirti, Mahakasyapa was able to adapt, unperturbed, to any and all situations and can be seen as a prototype for the expression of Chan mastery in the midst of ordinary life. He was also, however, responsible for undertaking the first internal critique of Buddhism, calling a council of Sangha elders to discuss the lax conduct of certain monks and nuns after the Buddha's death and to authorize a canon of the Buddha's teachings (Dharma) and communal regulations (Vinaya). Indeed, although the Buddha explicitly refused to authorize anyone to lead the Buddhist community after his own death, Mahakasyapa was often referred to as the "father of the Sangha."

Given Chan's claim with respect to other forms of Buddhism in China, all these qualities would have been important. But certainly, Mahakasyapa's particular karmic background must have factored into his adoption as first ancestor. In nineteen of his lives that are recounted in the *Jataka Tales* of the Buddha's own prior lives, Mahakasyapa was a close relative of the Buddha-to-be; in six, he was the future Buddha's father. This family connection would have resonated strongly with the Chinese disposition for seeing all relationships in familial terms. But, in addition, Mahakasyapa was unique among the Buddha's closest disciples in that he did not embark on his spiritual quest as a lone deserter of the home life. Instead, he did so with his wife—a woman who matched his ideals and shared his commitment to discovering a way of finally resolving all suffering. Meeting great social resistance to traveling together—a man and woman—as spiritual seekers, they decided to separate, vowing that whoever was the first to awaken under a good teacher should then find the other. As it happened, both found their way to the Buddha and realized full liberation under his guidance.

Granted the long-standing Chinese denunciation of Buddhist clergy as nonfilial, Mahakasyapa's strong family karma would not have been incidental. Among the Buddha's other closest disciples, the two most respected—Sariputra and Mahamoggallana—were known respectively as the "marshal of the Dharma" and the "master of psychic powers." Mahakasyapa demonstrated a socially viable middle way between the scholar and the mystic—one capable of bringing about communal harmony and a sense of familial care and respect even among literal strangers. Adept at responding within social situations, loyal to his parents and teachers, capable of questioning authority and authoring the creative extension of tradition, Mahakasyapa exemplified precisely the kind of Buddhist mastery required in the crucial years of the late Tang and Five Dynasties period.

As the narrative of Mahakasyapa's silent transmission from the Buddha came to enjoy canonical status, Chan's insistence on the ultimate authority of a silent transmission outside the teachings was effectively legitimated. Along with this acceptance came a spiritual imperative to realize the meaning of Mahakasyapa's smile—the simple gesture that had earned him a direct transmission of the Buddha's awakened mind. As Chinese Buddhists came to accept the reality of their own homegrown buddhas, it was only natural that this imperative be extended to the more immediate enlightening relationships between Chinese Chan masters and their students.

These elements of Chan led to the birth of new genres of Buddhist writing in China: "flame histories" and discourse records; encounter dialogues *(wenda);* and, finally, the famous Chan *gongan,* or "public cases." These recordings of the sayings and teachings of Chan masters, their dramatic relationships with students, and their condensation and compilation as public cases of liberating intimacy became the primary resources on which Chan advocacy drew and through which the tradition evolved. They also became concrete avenues by means of which there took place a meaningful accommodation of Chan within Chinese culture, particularly in the early to mid–Song dynasty. Indeed, it is now clear that the literary golden age of Chan occurred in the eleventh and twelfth centuries, not in the almost mythically creative period of the Tang.

Some contemporary scholars conclude from this fact that Chan virtually invented itself in the early Song, writing its history in an outburst of collective, creative genius in response to the practical necessity of earning economic and social patronage in the new society of the Song. This conclusion seems to me an unfortunate consequence of enforcing current academic standards of external or objective evidence in the study of Chan.

The internal Chan view has been that the literary explosion of the Song stands as evidence of a degeneration of the tradition. Since it is a tradition self-consciously rooted in the impossibility of capturing the meaning of enlightenment in words and letters, this view seems entirely self-consistent. Because it is a tradition that insisted as well on the personal demonstration of responsive virtuosity and the relational expression of truly liberating intimacy among all things, it also seems self-consistent that instances of such demonstrations would become a well-rehearsed and central part of Chan's communal lore.

That these instances would only much later be formalized in written form is no more difficult to understand than the similar history of standards in improvised forms of music like blues and jazz. These standards were played, embellished, and transmitted for several generations before being committed to writing and subjected to musical analysis. Many blues and jazz traditionalists saw this objectification of the music as the first signs that it had begun dying—a death that was averted, some would argue, only by the infusion of the tradition with new instruments for making these unique kinds of music. Similarly, it seems reasonable that Chan improvisations of enlightening relationships flourished for the better part of a century in the complete absence of any written scores and that the commission of these to writing—initially in the strict idiom of the classical Chinese scholar—was first perceived as the beginning of the end. The classical language was quickly turned to other uses, blended with vernacular narrative structures and tropes, and gave rise to a renaissance of Chan sensibilities as expressed in the written form.

In either case, it remains clear that the advocacy of Chan was undertaken first and foremost in the most deeply personal of ways.

The traditional Five Houses of Chan were, indeed, "family" lineages rooted in the personal transmission of the character of Chan awakening. Although only the Linji and Caodong lines would survive beyond the Song, it is the utterly intimate nature of Chan teaching that has allowed Chan Buddhism to continue flourishing not only throughout the Song dynasty and in the late Ming and Qing dynasties, but also on to the present day in both Asia and the West.

The transmission of Chan sensibilities takes place as virtuosic teachers immerse themselves in exemplary relationships with their students, teaching with words but certainly not through them. If the traditional accounts are to be respected, then there is no alternative but to admit that the communication taking place among Chan masters and their students has never consisted primarily of an exchange of information but of the realization of an almost musical resonance—a shared spirit of enlightening endeavor. Short of entering into such a relationship, the only means of addressing this spirit is to attune oneself, as fully as possible, to the traditionally expressed narrative rhythms of living Chan.

CHAPTER 5

Exemplars of Chan, Homegrown Buddhas

The spirit of living Chan is intensely personal. This spirit is made most clear in the tradition's renunciation of text-centered modes of authority and its insistence, instead, on the sole authority of a direct and active demonstration of our own, original buddha-nature. More subtly, it is evidenced in Chan's shift away from fixed teachings about how things are or should be to improvised teaching relationships through which the meaning of an entire situation is skillfully redirected. Indeed, Chan awakening can be described as the realization of dramatic and liberating intimacy with and among all things.

Because of these qualities, the spirit of Chan is most fully expressed in the life stories of eminent masters and their students. Even today, Chan practitioners consider the central characters in these stories to be—in a quite literal sense—their teachers. Here, I will focus on just four exemplary teachers in the traditional lineage that runs from Bodhidharma through Huineng, Mazu, and Linji. The stories of these seminal masters and the glimpses they afford of Chan teaching relationships strikingly capture both the spiritual force of Chan and the meaningful advent of unprecedented, "homegrown" buddhas on Chinese soil.

Bodhidharma

Of all the Indian and Central Asian monks who made their way into China, Bodhidharma is far and away the most famous. His spiritual legacy runs so wide and so deep that even today he is invoked daily by Chan and Zen teachers encouraging their students to follow his example in single-mindedly cutting through to the heart of the matter of life and death.

Bodhidharma is revered as the twenty-eighth holder of a direct line of transmission from the Buddha himself. As already noted, the traditional lineage began when Mahakasyapa correctly intuited the meaning of the Buddha's gesture of holding aloft a single flower during a public teaching. Not relying on words and letters, the Buddha's raised flower and Mahakasyapa's smile set a precedent for directly demonstrating the mind-with-mind resonance of enlightening communication. True to his lineage, Bodhidharma was not given to wordy explanations and expositions. There are only a small handful of texts that purport to recall Bodhidharma's teachings, and of these only one is generally considered authentic—a document only a few pages in length.

On the basis of so little information, why is Bodhidharma so widely and deeply revered? The obvious answer is that he directly links the Chinese tradition of Chan and the historical Buddha. But the same could be said of any ordained Buddhist and any sutra. By some route, all monks and nuns can trace a spiritual genealogy back to the early followers gathered around the Buddha. The words in every sutra can be traced back to a teaching delivered by the Buddha himself. Bodhidharma's special status does not lie in the simple fact of his direct line back to the Buddha but in the quality of his personification of the Buddha's enlightening presence.

The traditional story is that Bodhidharma was the third son of a south Indian king of the warrior caste. At a banquet hosted by his father, the young Bodhidharma meets an east Indian Buddhist teacher named Prajnatara. Of all the teachers invited to the banquet, Prajnatara is the only one who does not quote from the sutras and sastras. Tracing his lineage back to Mahakasyapa, Prajnatara represents a line of transmission beyond texts and treatises. He takes Bodhidharma as a disciple, passing on his robe and bowl as symbols of Bodhidharma's direct link back to the Buddha himself. He also charges Bodhidharma with a mission: traveling to China and spreading the Dharma, or true teaching, there.

Bodhidharma travels by sea from India through the islands of Southeast Asia and up the coast of China. Sometime near the end of the fifth or early in the sixth century c.e., he disembarks near modern-day Canton. In relatively short order, he is introduced to the court of the Liang dynasty, where he has several encounters with Emperor Wu —one of the most prolific patrons of Buddhism in Chinese history. In the most famous of these meetings, Emperor Wu asks Bodhidharma about the true meaning of Buddhism. Bodhidharma responds from the Mahayana perspective of the "perfection of wisdom" tradition: as the teachings of the buddhas and bodhisattvas are expressions of emptiness, how can they be caught in the web of true and false?

Emperor Wu is taken aback by this response and asks, then, about the merit he has made by sponsoring the building of temples, the translation of scriptures, the ordination of monks and nuns, and the institution of social welfare projects. Bodhidharma's answer is even more confounding: no merit at all. The emperor is deeply disturbed. One anecdote has it that he tries to get a definitive rise out of Bodhidharma by remarking that he has a nose like that of a pig. Bodhidharma is said to have replied that, as all things originally have no essential self-nature, whether a nose is piglike or not is a function of the karma being made by the perceiver, not the perceived.

This reply does not sit well with the emperor. Bodhidharma is sharp enough to realize that he is not making headway with the emperor and is, instead, likely to endanger his own life and mission by continuing in this vein. He leaves the court, crosses the Yangzi River, and heads north. Taking up residence not far from the Shaolin temple on Mount Song and near the northeastern capital of Luoyang, Bodhidharma spends nine years practicing a form of meditation referred to as "wall-gazing" or "wall-like gazing."

No straightforward explanation is given for this term. It is possible that it simply referred to the literal practice of facing a wall while sitting in meditation. Some contemporary schools of Japanese Zen do precisely this as a way of recalling Bodhidharma's profound determination and as a way of minimizing sensory distractions. Alternatively, the term could mean meditating in such a way that one loses the experience of having a particular point of view that shifts from one thing to another. Instead of gazing as an individual subject onto an objective world, one is to maintain a pointless perspective, attending "wall-like" to all things at once.

What is clear from descriptions of the effect of Bodhidharma's practice of meditation is that it dissolves the root of all polarities. Is and is-not, true and false, self and other, sage and commoner, and merit-making and sin all fall away. Meditation quiets or pacifies the mind. In the tradition traced back to Bodhidharma, this pacification is not a function of restricting the free play of awareness or of closing it off from full contact with the world. Instead, meditation quiets practitioners through emptying us of the basis for picking and choosing, for wavering between alternatives and doubting. Originally, Chan meditation is a way of abiding in utter clarity about our nature and direction, cutting entirely through our habit of relying on verbal teachings and establishing goals to be reached.

When Bodhidharma teaches the pacification of the mind through meditation, his Chinese students do not understand this to mean a quieting only of thought processes. The Chinese term used by Bodhidharma and all future generations of Chan Buddhists is *"xin."* Although it can be translated as "mind" (as, for brevity's sake, I have generally chosen to do here), the written character actually depicts a human heart and refers to a functional nexus of bodily forces, thoughts, and emotions. *Xin* is thus heart-mind, and its pacification means realizing the dramatic stillness of a thoroughly poised awareness.

Paintings and ink drawings of Bodhidharma—one of the most common subjects in Buddhist religious art in East Asia—typically show a hulking and bearded Caucasian man, often sitting in meditation or crossing the Yangzi River on his way north. His eyebrows are as thick and dark as thunderclouds, and his eyes are almost invariably wide open and glaring, directly meeting the viewer's gaze. Clearly, a quiet heart-mind in the Chan sense is not sleepy or blank. Bodhidharma's pointed stare bristles with energy, as if his eyebrows were colliding to send flashes of lightning precisely in the viewer's direction. It is an unmoving stare that manages somehow never to miss a thing.

In the one text generally agreed to summarize Bodhidharma's teaching, two "entrances" to the Buddhist path are discussed: principle and practice. Entering through principle means encountering the Buddha's teachings and giving rise to a deep and unshakable confidence that all living beings manifest one true nature. With this confidence, practicing wall-gazing meditation and abiding in unwavering presence means directly realizing horizonless nonduality.

The Chinese term used by Bodhidharma is only poorly translated by "principle" or "reason." Early uses of the term were in the context of dividing land into areas for cultivation according to natural topography. Including the graph for "jade" in its written form, the term was also used to refer to the grain patterns in natural stone and wood. Such features express the distinctive character of particular stones or pieces of wood and must be carefully taken into account when being shaped or crafted. That is, the patterning in a stone or a piece of wood is at once a record of its conditioned arising and a portrait of natural dispositions according to which it can be transformed.

Like such generative patterns of relating, the "principle" of Bodhidharma's teaching consists of opening oneself to the patterns of relationship or interdependence obtaining among all things and seeing in these patterns their one true nature. This is not a process of identifying some identical substance or essence in each thing but of recognizing that they participate in a shared meaning, each uniquely contributing to a profoundly common movement. Entering the path by way of principle or patterning is actively realizing partnership with all things.

Jewelers do not oppose the patterning of jade but rather work with it. Wood carvers are not limited by wood grain but experience it as a crucial contribution to that dance of materials, tools, bodily movements, and sentiments that is called artistic creativity. The "principle" of nonduality does not entail eliminating differences but only conflict and compartmentalization. It means refraining from either rejecting things or clinging to them. Rejecting and clinging deny the meaning of differences as openings for mutual contribution. They assert separateness and reduce the interdependence of all things to, at best, mere coexistence. Nonduality means closing the wound of existence.

In this sense, entering the path by way of "principle" is a form of practice—it is something confidently done or demonstrated. It is not a mere belief in certain "facts" about the world or an assent to authoritative ideals from which human beings are always once removed. Thus, Bodhidharma clearly states that the entrance of "principle" cannot be experienced secondhand, even through the most sacred scriptures. Following after words and letters is like studying markings on the gate of wisdom without ever throwing it open. Entrance by principle means freely passing beyond both the sufficient and the insufficient, confidently seeing all things as patterned toward liberating relationships.

Appreciating the nonduality of things is given concrete purchase in day-to-day life through entrance by "practice." The term translated here as "practice"—*xing*—is a powerful one in Chinese thought. Its root meanings are "to walk" and "to do," but it also implies creating a path, establishing a series, and acting in concert. When used as a component in writing more complex words, these words typically imply meaningful interchange and movement—words like "thoroughfare" and "marketplace." In this sense, the basic practice implied by the word "*xing*" is that of opening pathways for sharing or mutual contribution. Thus, in the correlative cosmology assumed by both Confucianism and Daoism, "*xing*" was used to refer to the five archetypal configurations of energy, or *qi:* the five elemental courses or basic qualitative flows through which all things are connected. Finally, in the translation of Indian Buddhist texts, "*xing*" was used to render both habit formations and the cultivation of practices that dissolve ignorance, habit, and clinging desires to open one onto wisdom, attentive virtuosity, and moral clarity.

Overall, "*xing*" implies a continuum stretching from the activity of bringing about habitually directed relationships to conduct that frees one from any preestablished relational courses. In the "gates" of the Middle Path, *xing* functions as "hinges" or "pivots." Not surprisingly, there is a focus on skillfully working with karma in the four practices Bodhidharma discusses: accepting apparent injustice, corresponding with present conditions, seeking nothing, and expressing the Dharma for the benefit of others.

The very first noble truth of Buddhism is that, in any situation, from some perspective, there is trouble. There is no life in which trouble and adversity do not occur. Most of us, as soon as trouble and adversity arise, think that they are not our fault and do our best to reject or counter them. We believe that they are imposed on us by chance or destiny or the ill intentions of others. Not only is resisting our right; we believe it is right to do so. Bodhidharma recommends otherwise. He suggests in the *Long Scroll of the Treatise on the Two Entrances and Four Practices,* that we practice thinking in the following way:

From the past, over countless lifetimes, I have become unaware of the roots [originating conditions] and followed after the branches [effects]. I have passed from one form of existence to another, producing a lot of ill will and hatred, bothering and hurting others without end. Although I've apparently done nothing wrong in this present case, this trouble and suffering are the ripening of unfortunate karmic fruits from transgressions in past lives. It is not something visited on me by either the gods or men. I bear and accept it openly, with no complaint.

Bodhidharma's suggestion has to be understood in the context of the Mahayana Buddhist directive of saving all beings from suffering, including ourselves. The practice of accepting apparent injustice is not one of simply giving in to one's circumstances and suffering whatever comes one's way. Our responsibility is to resolve all suffering meaningfully. But this cannot be done if one's first step is that of denying intimacy with one's situation as well as responsibility for being present within it.

A sadly common example of the consequences of such a denial can be seen in what is now popularly referred to as a "codependent relationship." To the continued surprise of family members and friends, the people locked into such a relationship are often incapable of seeing how destructive their interactions are. Often, they seem blind to the most obvious facts of their own situation, typically believing that everything will change for the better once something changes in their circumstances—a new job, a new house, a new baby, a vacation or a break. They cannot see that their own actions feed the cycle of negativity that is choking them emotionally, blocking out any opportunity for growth and fostering their sense of being down on their luck. The only apparent "solution" is to leave the relationship and find a new and better partner—a partner who tragically and "against all odds" turns out to be precisely the same sort of person as the last. People prone to such destructive codependence often experience themselves as the victims of fate, as simply not being able to help themselves.

The second practice recommended by Bodhidharma is refusing to block out or disown one's present situation. This practice not only holds open intimate connections with the other things and beings present together with us, it brings about an ongoing awareness of one's capacity to change the nature of one's contribution to the situation—to revise its meaning even if the totality of its facts lie beyond one's immediate control. By accepting any presently apparent injustice, one takes at least partial responsibility for how things are going, seeing oneself as an integral part of the situation and not a helpless victim of it. The present moment is never simply inflicted on us by "others"—whether divine beings, humans, or impersonal forces like chance or fate or scientific law. It is a shared dramatic field that is intrinsically open and responsive—the result of patterns of interaction rooted in our own intentions and values. Precisely because this is so, the troubles and adversity we experience are not intractable: we are always in a position to contribute to their meaningful resolution. By refusing to disown our situation, we effectively avoid being caught by or trapped in it.

Granted the conditioned arising and impermanence of all things, even the best situations will not last forever. Holding onto or clinging to what one believes is a "good situation" is just as problematic as blindly rejecting one seen as "bad." It marks a refusal to be fully present, attentive to the changing dynamics of one's situation, and actualizing the harmonious interplay of differences that is nonduality. Holding onto a situation—trying to freeze it into lasting, perhaps forever—is to deny that the changes now taking place contribute to the overall meaning of things in complete accordance with their one true nature: a disposition toward liberation. Corresponding with present conditions is actively maintaining nonduality.

The first two practices by means of which Bodhidharma says we can enter the Buddhist path focus on seeing things karmically. Their point is to dissolve tendencies toward rejecting and clinging. These practices involve becoming attuned to the "causal roots" of each situation in such a way as to realize full nonduality with it—seeing it as expressing a shared past karma. The third practice—seeking nothing—opens a way toward freeing the future of any duality. Not seeking anything means having no fixed goals or destinations.

The first impulse in hearing this is likely to be denial. How can we live without any goals, with nothing to attain or dream of achieving? Why go from one day to the next if not to get what we want or to become who we want? For Bodhidharma, the problem is not what we want or who we want to be but the process of wanting. The teaching of emptiness instructs us to see all things as having no fixed or essential nature—seeing them, that is, as not being inherently good, bad, or (even) neutral. So a car is not inherently a good or bad thing to want. Doctors, professional entertainers, and soldiers are neither inherently good nor inherently bad types of people to be. Wanting, however, means being in want or lacking something. It means being not yet complete, not yet full, not yet satisfied. Setting something up as a goal or destination announces separation from it. Wanting and seeking deny interdependence and nonduality.

There are no destinations in the absence of a clear separation between a wanting subject and a wanted object. There must be an intervening space that holds apart the one who wants and that which is wanted. Bodhidharma does not urge us to refrain from seeking because we are doomed to fail but because of the full meaning of doing so successfully. First, there is the karma created by wanting and getting what one wants. This is not simply a line from start to finish. It is a circular track. Thus, the better we get at getting what we want, the better we get at wanting; but the better we get at wanting, the better we get at getting what we want, though we won't want what we get. The karma of wanting is an ever-intensifying cycle of perceived poverty and apparent satisfaction.

Given that the feeling of being in want or lacking something is always troubling, this would seem good reason to resist setting up goals and destinations. But what if what we want most of all is enlightenment or liberation? Isn't that a goal worth wanting? Bodhidharma's answer is a resounding "no!"—a response that is later taken up by the Chan tradition as a whole and that reaches its rhetorical limit with Linji and his iconoclastic claim that "should you meet 'the Buddha' on the road, kill him!" Bodhidharma does not appeal to the language of "sudden" and "gradual" paths of enlightenment that would eventually dominate Chan discussions of the problem of establishing "enlightenment" as a goal. Instead, he focuses on the incompatibility of seeking and of confidently actualizing the nonduality of our one true nature.

"People of this world," he says, "are in a whirling pattern of delusion. They are always wanting for something—perpetually seeking.

Persons of insight awaken truth. Principle grasped and conventions overthrown, with a pacified heart-mind and unprecedented conduct their forms follow the turnings of the world and the ten thousand things empty." For Bodhidharma, not seeking means seeing that, finally, there is nothing to grasp or lack since there are no things from which we are inherently separated. Not seeking anything means, then, participating freely in the interdependence and emptiness of all things.

Negatively described, this means accepting what is now happening, refraining from judging or resisting it. That, however, is just a means of removing karmic blockages. More positively, it means awakening from duality and dispelling the obstructing dream of permanently having what we want and not having what we do not want. When the ten thousand things empty, there is no longer anything in them to "offer" us resistance. They will be freed from being placed (by us) in the position of forcing us to realize the extent of our patterns of ignorance and restriction. In such a liberated situation, all things—each one of us included—are enabled simply to do what needs to be done to express our one true nature.

The final practice recommended by Bodhidharma is "invoking and tallying with the teaching that the generative pattern of all natures is pure and purifying." Since all forms and characteristics are empty, abiding in unobstructed interdependence, they are without defilement, without attachment, neither essentially this nor that. "Those who are able to confidently actualize this teaching and practice according to it realize that embodying the teachings is being without stinginess. They offer body, life, and possessions with minds free of grudging and regret. . . . For the simple purpose of departing from impurity, they embrace and transform sentient beings without grasping after characteristics." Practicing like this benefits both others and oneself, and adorns the path to liberation.

Embracing and transforming sentient beings is precisely the work performed by the Buddha over the course of his teaching career—a career that began with his determination to offer others guidance toward sharing his insight into the Middle Way. It is for this reason that Bodhidharma refers to this final practice as "expressing the Dharma." The true medium for expressing the Dharma is not language but the teaching relationship.

If the third practice urges us to refrain from seeking anything and breaking with our karma for wanting, the fourth practice involves us in actively replacing goals and destinations with a clear direction: embarking wholeheartedly on the path of offering. In Mahayana Buddhism, reference is often made to six *paramitas*, or modes of perfection, that will enable us to turn away from the conflicts and trouble of samsara toward the joyous liberation of nirvana. These are wisdom, meditation, zealousness, patience, moral clarity, and gift giving or offering. Bodhidharma claims—as will many Chan masters after him —that, if the practice of offering is perfected, all the other *paramitas* will be practiced and perfected as well.

Like the karma of wanting, the karma of gift giving or offering is cyclic. But it is a very different sort of cycle. It begins with perceiving an opportunity to contribute to things in some specific way—either addressing a particular need or adding to the value of what is already present. The better we get at perceiving such opportunities, however, the more we experience being in a position to do so. Seeing more opportunities to offer what is needed or what will enrich our situation also means having more and more of what is needed, more and more with which to enrich others and our situation. As our karma for offering or giving matures, we find that the more we are able to give, the more we are enabled to give. Increasing opportunities for offering imply increasing resources for doing so.

It is for this reason that Bodhidharma insists that there is no separation between benefiting others, benefiting oneself, and adorning the path of awakening. And it is why he insists that the perfection of giving brings about as well the perfection of wisdom, meditation, zeal, patience, and moral clarity. As one's karma for offering develops, one will naturally develop a more and more refined understanding of the interdependence of all things and how to meaningfully contribute to it. In short, one will develop wisdom: fuller and fuller insight into the emptiness or mutual relevance of all things and the resources they afford for offering. This means as well perfecting meditation: an increasing capacity for open and responsively attuned awareness. It means having the energy and unwavering motivation to act as needed, when needed: the perfection of zeal or vigor. It means sensitivity to timing and a capacity for acting only when and as needed: the development of patience. Finally, it means being able to see what must be done to redirect a situation dramatically: developing sufficient moral clarity to see how to contribute meaningfully to the liberating revision of troubled relationships.

For Chan, it is crucial that bestowing gifts or offering is not a process of making merit. It is not a matter of doing things in order to receive a particular compensation or to bring about a particular desired state of affairs. Bodhidharma's Chan lies far away from such calculations of utility. The four practices that he recommends establish a spiral movement out of pointlike awareness of being the victim of a "bad" situation to the relinquishing of all horizons to what we have to offer.

It is not coincidental that the culminating life in the series of births leading up to the Buddha's enlightenment as Siddhartha Gautama is that of Prince Vessantara—a life centered on the perfection of giving. Nor is it coincidental that the layman Vimalakirti—whose rhetorical skills and wisdom were so deeply appreciated by the Chinese—described our present world realm, the Buddha's home realm, as one in which all things (even "bad" odors and "deplorable" conditions) do the great work of enlightenment. Offering is the key to unlocking the resources within our present moment for swinging open the gates of liberation and restoring all things to their one true nature.

In combination, the entrances of "principle" and "practice" usher us into realizing that no boundaries lie between us and liberation. In a record of questions and answers associated with Bodhidharma and his circle of students, someone asks, "Where is the place of enlightenment?" The answer echoes the *Vimalakirti Sutra:* "The place you are walking on is the place of enlightenment; the place you are lying on is the place of enlightenment; the place you are sitting is the place of enlightenment; the place your are standing is the place of enlightenment. Wherever you pick up your feet or put them down—that is the place of enlightenment!" There can be no more unequivocal rejection of the idea that enlightenment is somewhere far away in time or space, something attained by others under circumstances not our own.

The conception and birth of Chan pivots on taking this absence of blockages to liberation utterly in earnest. In the same record of questions and answers, it is said that "the energy *(qi)* of those who attain a realization through the medium of written words is weak; those who attain realization from their own circumstances and events will have robust energy. Seeing the Dharma in the medium of events means never losing mindfulness anywhere." The many portraits of Bodhidharma suggest precisely this robust energy and unshakable attentiveness—a presence that cuts through all complications and confusions to reveal the possibility, here and now, of awakening.

Huineng

Bodhidharma, the first Chan patriarch or ancestral teacher, had but a handful of disciples. Tradition has it that Huike—a well-educated, one-armed monk from a good family—received Bodhidharma's robe and bowl in material proof of an uninterrupted line of transmission extending back to the Buddha himself. Although there is no contemporary evidence of it, later Chan legend has it that he cut his arm off in demonstration of his sincerity, offering it to Bodhidharma in return for his teaching—a model instance of unflinching determination to enter the family of the patriarchs.

Four generations later, the fifth patriarch, Hongren, transmitted this robe and bowl to an illiterate layman named Huineng. In symbolic confirmation that the Buddha's mind seal had indeed taken root in China and no longer needed foreign confirmation, when Huineng died, Bodhidharma's robe and bowl were sealed into his tomb. From this point on, Buddhist enlightenment in China would be confidently homegrown.

Unlike Bodhidharma, whose teachings are veritably recorded in only a small handful of texts, an extended record of teachings attributed to Huineng began circulating sometime in the century following his death in 713 C.E. Contemporary scholars continue to debate the origins and historical accuracy of this record—*The Platform Sutra of Huineng*—and the extent to which the teachings contained in it can be traced back to Huineng himself. These debates, however, have little to do with the spiritual force of Huineng's legacy as the sixth patriarch of Chan. By the middle of the ninth century, the spiritual genealogy of every Chan lineage holder would include Huineng and his teaching of "sudden" awakening through seeing one's own nature.

The *Platform Sutra* opens with Huineng very briefly relating his life story. In the literature of Buddhism up to this time, such an auto-biographical introduction presents an entirely unprecedented image. Huineng stands before an assembly of hundreds of people and speaks not of some arcane aspect of Buddhist philosophy or of a profound passage from the sutras, but of his own very humble and very human origins. Although it would become common for short remarks about teachers' lineages and places of residence to be appended to their discourse records, Huineng himself goes into considerable detail in establishing his completely ordinary Chinese roots.

His father was a minor official who was dismissed from his post for undisclosed reasons and banished to live as a commoner in a rural backwater. When Huineng was three, his father died, leaving his mother to raise him on her own. She moved with her toddler to Nanhai—the port in which Bodhidharma is reputed to have made landfall in his journey from India. There mother and son lived in abject poverty.

As a fatherless child, Huineng soon took on adult responsibilities, gathering firewood to sell to travelers staying at various nearby inns. Sometime in his mid-twenties, Huineng was carrying a load of fire-wood when he heard a customer at one of the inns reciting a verse from the *Diamond Sutra.* Huineng dropped his load in astonishment. It was as if the verse was a key that unlocked a door he had never thought present for him. What Huineng saw through that opening moved him so deeply that he decided to leave Nanhai in search of a spiritual master.

According to a biography compiled in the first decades after his death, Huineng wanders into the countryside and is soon introduced to a Buddhist nun devoted to the *Nirvana Sutra.* She recites passages for him, and asks him to take a turn reading aloud from the sutra. He tells her that he cannot. He has never learned to read. She is amazed. How can he hope to understand the sutras—the discourses of the Buddha himself—if he cannot even read? Huineng replies that the body of buddha-nature is not made up of words and letters, so what need should there be for deciphering texts? She and her fellow vil-lagers are impressed with his retort and suggest that he embark on the homeless life of Buddhist monk. Huineng does not leave the lay life at this point, but he does undertake meditative training under the tutelage of a local meditation master.

After three years of training in a mountain cave, Huineng travels to East Mountain, where he meets the fifth Chan patriarch, Hongren. The master asks Huineng where he is from, why he has come to East Mountain, and what he is looking for from him. Huineng replies that he is a commoner who has come simply to bow to Hongren and ask for Buddhist teachings. Hongren is said to have snorted derisively. "If you're from the deep south as you say, then you're a barbarian"—literally, something between a wild animal and a human. "How could you ever become a buddha?"

Huineng is not taken aback by the insult. He admits that there is a difference between people from the north and the south. But "in buddha-nature, there is no north and south. Although my 'barbarian' body and yours differ, what difference is there in our buddha-nature?" Hongren inwardly recognizes Huineng's great promise but, considering the politics of the monastery, publicly dismisses him. Later, he has a lay disciple take Huineng to the threshing room, where he spends almost nine months in hard physical labor, treading the mill that separates rice kernels from their husks.

Huineng's story to this point makes a number of crucial points. He is not a member of the educated elite. As an illiterate, if he has any grounding in the Confucian and Daoist traditions, it is not based on knowledge of their texts but on how they are actually practiced. His life has not been one of privilege. Unlike Siddhartha Guatama, who lived in great luxury before departing on his quest for a solution to the problem of suffering, Huineng did not grow up as royalty or as an aristocrat for whom suffering was something distantly contemplated. As a tragically poor orphan in China, he would have seen the suffering of the human condition in full frontal view. He would have lived in the worst part of town and grown up associating with the elements of society that sink into the wharf areas and back alleys, the cheap inns and red light districts.

After more than two decades of hand-to-mouth existence, however, Huineng has not shut down. He has not been crushed into the deadening habits of society's castoffs—a population stooped under the immense burdens of poverty and withdrawn into self-protective ignorance. On the contrary, Huineng goes about his humble work with eyes and ears fully open. The fertility of his mind-ground *(xintu)* is such that when a stray verse from the *Diamond Sutra* falls on his ears, he has no doubt that his life has just changed direction—utterly and forever.

The *Diamond Sutra* is a "perfection of wisdom" text focused on the kind of attention that bodhisattvas must maintain if they are to do the work of liberating all beings from suffering. In it, the Buddha guides one of his most intellectually gifted students toward an affirmation of the emptiness of all things and the unlimited resources they offer. A constant refrain in the text is that what we take things or people to be tells us more about the quality and horizons of our own awareness than about anything else. The same tree can be a nuisance to one person and a comfort to another. The mold on a loaf of bread can be seen as something that will make us sick or as a potential cure (penicillin) for a host of bacteria-caused illnesses. Bodhisattvas must learn to see that a tree (the thing itself as a unique expression of the limitless interdependence of all things) is not a "tree" (that is, one's individual relationship with it, reflecting one's own patterns of ignorance and perceived relevance); we just refer to it as "a tree, a tree" (that is, by a particular, and in this case English, word). Failing to do so is failing to attend to the emptiness—and, therefore, mutual relevance—of all things. It is to close off resources, present in our immediate situation, for carrying out the great work of meaningfully resolving any and all suffering.

A central message of the *Diamond Sutra*—Huineng's wake-up call —is thus the need to attend to the nature of all things as open to doing the infinite buddha-work of enlightenment. But in the sutra, the Buddha clearly points out that, while bodhisattvas immeasurably enrich their situation by seeing all things in this way, they do not "get rich" themselves. When asked by Subhuti what he attained with the realization of "complete and unsurpassed awakening," the Buddha replies, "Not one single thing." Awakening is not a matter of getting anything —in the sense of a possession or a particular intellectual insight. Asked, then, what kind of awareness bodhisattvas should maintain, the Buddha responds: an awareness that does not rely on anything.

These teachings from the *Diamond Sutra* become central touchstones of Huineng's own teachings. His responses to the apparent insults of Hongren likewise become crucial pointers for the elemental spirit of Chan artlessness and spontaneity. Recalling Emperor Wu's attempt to insult Bodhidharma, Hongren's reference to Huineng as a "barbarian" is mirrored back as an opportunity for teaching the emptiness of all things—a way of concretely illustrating their shared disposition or nature of awakening. Thus, Huineng responds that Hongren is entirely correct in claiming differences between northerners and southerners but not in denying their shared buddha-nature. In this way, Huineng demonstrates how all things—even insults—can do the work of enlightenment. He does not "correct" Hongren with a self-defensive assertion of his "right" to study Chan. Nor does he deliver a sharp hammer blow from the pages of some Buddhist scripture. Instead, he responds to Hongren with unself-conscious emotional openness. First acknowledging the limited or conventional truth of Hongren's perspective, Huineng then asks a leading question—a question that invites Hongren at once to accept where he stands and to change the direction in which he is facing.

The fact that this exchange leads to Huineng being dispatched to the threshing room can be read in a number of ways. Knowing that he will eventually receive Hongren's robe and bowl and the title of sixth patriarch of Chan, Huineng's consignment to manual labor for nine months can be seen as an important "gestation" period. Huineng clearly shows that he has conceived the meaning of his own buddha-nature, but it has not yet been brought to the point of fruition. He has not yet learned to give birth to skilled bodhisattva action. Although his answer to Hongren's challenge marks him as a promising candidate for transmission, he is set to work refining that answer. It is one thing to harvest rice and another thing to make it appropriate for human consumption. Huineng's months in the threshing room are spent learning that responding as needed depends on first having accorded with the situation.

In the case of the monastery presided over by Hongren, the situation is at once spiritual and political. The story resumes when Hongren presents a challenge to the community. "You are all involved in making offerings for the purpose of planting a field of future blessings and are failing to seek a way beyond the ocean of cycling through the round of birth and death, good fortune and bad. With your own nature misdirected at the gate of blessings, how can you be saved? Return to your rooms; look into yourselves. Those who understand will grasp the wisdom *(prajna)* of their original nature" (*Platform Sutra,* section 7). He instructs his students to write individual verses that distill their understanding. He promises to read and evaluate each verse and to award his robe and the title of sixth patriarch to the most fully realized author.

The assembly files out in quiet turmoil. No one feels competent to do as asked, and all are confused by the sudden challenge that they demonstrate their understanding of Buddhist awakening. They decide to defer to the head monk, Shenxiu, allowing him to shoulder the responsibility of writing a proper verse and receiving Hongren's robe and teaching. In the *Platform Sutra,* Shenxiu spends the evening mulling over what to do: if he writes a verse, it will make it seem that he is arrogantly seeking the patriarchal robe and Dharma; but if he writes nothing, he will let down his fellow students and profit no one. He decides after midnight to sneak into a new meditation hall being built at the monastery and to write an anonymous verse on one of the new walls:

> The body is the *bodhi* tree.
> The heart-mind is like a bright mirror.
> Moment by moment wipe and polish it,
> Not allowing dust to collect.
> (*Platform Sutra,* section 6)

Shenxiu's verse is clear and to the point. The place of enlightenment, the *bodhi* tree, is one's own body. Enlightenment is not something that occurred once and for all under a banyan tree in India where Siddhartha Guatama sat for forty days in meditation. It can occur here and now. Our minds are like mirrors that are originally pure but are obscured by the dust of the world, appearing dull and unenlightened. Practice consists of polishing our minds, removing the impurities of the world, and allowing our original enlightenment to show.

The following day, Hongren reads the verse, calls the community together, and announces that they should all recite it in order to see into their own natures. Doing so, he tells them, will insure that they will not fall into ill-fated lives. After burning incense before the verse, Hongren asks Shenxiu to meet him privately. Shenxiu admits having written the verse and asks his master if there is in it even a shred of true understanding. Hongren allows that the verse shows that Shenxiu has reached the gate of true understanding. People who read it and practice in accord with it will keep from falling into grievous karmic patterns. But the verse also shows that Shenxiu has failed to enter and pass through the gate. He offers to let Shenxiu think about it for a few days and to write another verse worthy of the robe and Dharma that will make him the sixth patriarch of Chan.

While Shenxiu is struggling to understand his shortcomings, a young monk walks by the threshing room reciting his verse out loud. Huineng hears and realizes that the author has yet to understand his own true nature. He goes to the new dharma hall and has someone who can write for him place the following on the wall:

Bodhi originally has no tree.
The clear and bright mirror also has no support.
Buddha-nature is constantly purifying and clearing.
Where could there be dust?
(Platform Sutra, section 8)

With this verse, Huineng "hits" Shenxiu, aiming to bring his attention (and ours) around to the true meaning of our original nature.

The *Platform Sutra* represents Shenxiu as making two cardinal errors. First, he assumes that the locus of enlightenment is a subjective heart-mind that is contained and held up by the body much as a mirror is mounted in and supported by a stand. Second, he apparently assumes that at least some things and events in this world are inherently and objectively impure. Both mistakes rest on a failure to appreciate fully the meaning of the emptiness and interdependence of all things. Mind and body are treated as substantially existing and fundamentally separate entities—one bright and clearly reflective, the other dull and inert. Human nature, that is, is treated dualistically. If worldly things and experiences can obscure the enlightened heart-mind, then this duality extends to encompass our entire situation. The nature of the various impurities of the world must not only be fundamentally different than that of the enlightened heart-mind; they must be at least as original as it is. That is, all things do not express buddha-nature.

Huineng directly addresses the first error by maintaining that *bodhi* (awakening or enlightenment) has no fixed locus or point of origin. In other words, awakening does not take place. Since everything that comes to be also ceases to be, any awakening that takes place at a particular point in time and space cannot be original nature. This amounts to saying that awakening is not a purely objective and effectively limited event. But neither is it a purely subjective experience—something that happens to us as individuals. It cannot even be said that awakening dissolves the categories of subject and object. That would imply that they really exist and that the manifestation of our "original nature" depends on canceling them out.

Huineng denies the ultimate truth of any such dependent relationships by stating that the bright mirror—"mind" or "own nature"—has no stand or support. Since our individual experiences of a situation are always contingent on the acuity of bodily senses, the values according to which we interpret our sensory connections with things, and the karma that brings us into contact with these things and people and not those, our experience cannot be our original buddha-nature.

If that is so, then what is our own nature, our true mind? Huineng rejects the possibility that it is a nature that can be obscured or blocked. "Buddha-nature," he says, "is constantly purifying and clearing." This five-character line could also be read as "Buddha-nature is constantly pure and clear." This translation would suggest that buddha-nature, our original nature, is something that is essentially static or unchanging and is not impure or unclear. Buddha-nature would have to be interpreted as a state that literally transcends our lived world and perpetuates the duality of is and is-not. This would mean that buddha-nature fosters the "twin barbs on which all humankind is impaled"—the central causes of suffering. That is not acceptable.

Huineng clarifies by adding the final line, "Where could there be dust?" He does not state that buddha-nature cannot get dusty or dirtied by presence in the polluted realm of samsara. Such a statement would fail to address the problem of duality and would indirectly lead to its perpetuation. Instead, he challenges us to see that nothing like "dust" could possibly exist. Here, Huineng is echoing Vimalakirti's claim that in a buddha-realm, all things do the great work of enlightenment—all things express buddha-nature. It is not that our original nature is some inherently pristine essence. Rather, it is something actively done: the unfailingly continuous work of purifying and clearing. Thus, when asked to define what is meant by "Buddha," Huineng remarks that "it is precisely Buddhist conduct/practice that is Buddha." Practice is not a means to the end of enlightenment. It is the demonstration of our originally enlightening nature. Far from being a self-contained state achieved once and for all, it is an ongoing, transformative process. The Chan tradition embraces this notion with unrivaled intensity.

In a Chinese context, the term "nature" (xing) stresses patterns of relationship, activity, and energy. If our original nature is, indeed, buddha-nature; and if buddha-nature is, indeed, the ultimate meaning of interdependence or the practice of the Middle Path; then, our original nature consists of actively orienting relationships toward the meaningful resolution of suffering or trouble in the interdependence among all things. Given this, there can be no situation in which we cannot express our own nature.

This is the key to Huineng's famous teaching of so-called sudden enlightenment. Throughout the Platform Sutra, Huineng continuously characterizes his approach to teaching and practicing Buddhism as "sudden," not "gradual." He inherits the contrast from Chinese Buddhist commentarial traditions drawing on the work of second- and third-century Daoist writers who contrasted sudden and gradual expressions of the truth. The former refer to direct statements of meaning and the latter to indirect, metaphorical, or analogical ones. Chinese Buddhist scholars thus distinguished between teachings of the Buddha that were immediate and profound and those that relied on various "expedients" to guide people from shallow to deep expressions and understanding of Buddhist truth. The text-biased schools of Chinese Buddhism typically regarded their core scriptures as either "sudden" in just this sense or as "whole" and "complete." It was generally held that the most profound teachings of the Buddha were delivered to advanced audiences capable of sudden awakening. By contrast, teachings that relied on expedient means were for the sake of people requiring gradual cultivation before they would be capable of bearing the fruit of enlightenment.

Huineng makes it clear that he is not concerned with such objective differences in the verbal content of Buddhist teachings. "It is not the teachings that are sudden or gradual," he says, "but people who are keen or dull." The "sudden" teaching refers to a personally embodied quality, not to that of words and letters. At the same time, his stress on whether people are keen or dull is not intended to drive home a strictly temporal distinction. Huineng's point is not how long it takes people to awaken. His point is to stress qualitative differences in people's dispositions for awakening. Keen and dull roots distinguish between degrees of relational attunement and responsive acuity. The Chinese word translated as "keen" carries the connotations of being sharp, clever, profitable, or beneficial. It can also mean "gain," "advantage," or "interest." The sudden teaching for which Huineng is so famous is not a particular kind of doctrine but a particular kind of relationship—one that is precise, beneficial, and productive. The word translated as "dull" also means "blunt" or "stupid." The "gradual" approach to awakening is practiced by people without the attentive and dramatic resources needed to cut through the karmic tangles of cause and effect and reveal the true, enlightening nature of things just as they are.

Keen people have intentionally established the abilities and dispositions—the karmic "roots"—needed for spontaneously responding to things. They are able to use whatever is present as resources. People with dull roots are constrained by the use of familiar means and methods. They have not developed the abilities and dispositions needed for skillful improvisation. The distinction is neatly captured by the term typically translated as "sudden enlightenment" *(dunwu)*. *"Wu"* means to become aware, to awaken to, to perceive alertly. *"Dun"* can be translated as "sudden," but its root meanings are bowing the head, putting in order, preparing, or making ready. It refers to a dramatic turning point—the moment that a servant has bowed with forehead to the ground, received the master's directives, and is rising to go into action. Similarly, conducting ourselves as bodhisattvas involves humbly exhibiting an unalloyed readiness to be of service in the realization of awakening.

The meaning of Huineng's use of *"dunwu"* is thus only partially and rather poorly captured by the term "sudden enlightenment." More accurately, *"dunwu"* might be rendered as "readiness to awaken" or "readiness for awakening." The ambiguity of this phrase works well in rendering the Chinese into English. It accurately leaves unclear whether you yourself are ready to awaken, whether you are ready to awaken someone else, or whether we are all poised in a situation that is itself ready for awakening. Especially as understood in Chan, the Buddhist teaching of nonduality invites us to practice refraining from the selfishness of existence or "standing apart from" all others. It is an invitation to see that, if all things are truly interdependent and empty, there is no ultimate warrant for talking about "my enlightenment" or "your suffering." Such terms only reinforce the conceit that "I am" (separate and independent of "you")—a way of insuring that we continue to oscillate between is and is-not rather than embarking in earnest on the Middle Way. Indeed, as Huineng insists, "our own nature contains the myriad things; the myriad things exhaustively constitute own nature." Seeing our own nature is seeing the utter continuity of the interdependence or mutual contribution obtaining among all things. We are not, in any sense, outside-standers. We do not transcend or exist independently of our situation and all that it comprises.

Huineng's teaching of the "readiness to awaken" thus exhorts us to guard vigilantly against setting up awakening as a goal to be sought. Practicing nonduality, we cannot assume that meditation is a method for arriving at the goal of wisdom. Meditation and wisdom, Huineng insists, form a single whole.

Asked what he means by "sitting in meditation," Huineng answers that "'sitting' means without any obstruction at all, outwardly and in all situations, not to give rise to thinking; 'meditation' is internally to see original nature and not become confused." It is a mistake to think that Chan sitting meditation consists of sitting without moving, casting away delusions, and not allowing any thoughts to arise. Practicing like this is the same as being dead or insentient and is a blockage on the Middle Path of interdependence. The pattern of all things—the Dao—must be allowed to circulate freely. Huineng asks, "If sitting in meditation without moving is good, why did Vimalakirti scold Sariputra for sitting in meditation in the woods?" If the function of meditation is wisdom, how can meditation consist of sitting alone in the forest, absorbed in contemplation?

For Indian Buddhists, wisdom, or *prajna,* was defined by "knowledge of the waning of influxes." It meant realizing a state of consciousness free from impure influences and defiling activity. Chinese Buddhists generally rendered *prajna* with *"zhihui,"* a compound word literally meaning "realizing quick wittedness or prudence." Wisdom is not a matter of knowing about the nature of things or realizing the cessation of unhealthy influences, but of responsive virtuosity. Huineng leaves no doubt about the meaning and character of this contributory brilliance. In the *Platform Sutra,* the usual character meaning clever or prudent is replaced by another (also pronounced *"hui"*) that means "conferring kindness," "benefit," "favor," "according with," and "being gracious." For Huineng, the function of meditation is skilled offering in a spirit of understanding kindness.

Chan meditation involves "at all times, whether walking, standing, sitting, or lying down, continually practicing and conducting yourself with authentic heart and mind" (*Platform Sutra,* section 14). Huineng refers to this idea with a phrase that can be translated as the "single-practice *samadhi,*" the "whole-conduct *samadhi,*" or the "one-course *samadhi.*" The one necessary and sufficient element of Chan practice is realizing clear and unobstructed attentive virtuosity. If we are able to "give rise to wisdom *(zhihui)* and shine *(zhao)* with it," nothing else is necessary.

The Chinese term *(zhao)* used by Huineng to describe the activity of wisdom has the connotation of "illuminating," "reflecting," or "shining" but also "to look after" or "care for." Contrary to Shenxiu's verse, Huineng makes it clear that Chan awakening is not a matter of dusting off one's own mind but of immediately shining or polishing one's situation to the point of brilliance. But if Shenxiu errs in suggesting that our own minds must be cleared of dust, it is just as much of an error to imagine that the purpose of wisdom is wiping away "dust" —the pall of impurity—that has settled on the things in our environment. With iconoclastic fervor, Huineng denies that there is any "dust" at all.

In conventional Buddhist terms, our human passions are among the most binding and obscuring kind of dust. But for Huineng they are not inherently so. "Good friends," he announces (*Platform Sutra*, section 26), "it is precisely the passions that awaken. . . . If you hold onto or are caught by a past moment or thinking of it and are then seduced into error—that is being a commoner. Awakening in the very next thought or moment is being a buddha. If past thinking has made horizons manifest, that is 'passion.' If your next thought relinquishes all horizons, then that is 'awakening.'" As we are always present, the choice of direction is ours. If we see things as resisting our wills, as obstructing our path, as impediments to awakening, they form horizons beyond which we cannot see. What we see does not provide evidence of their original nature, however, but only of our own ignorance. Horizons do not really exist. They are simply functions of our limited point of view, reflecting our narrow perspective, our inability to see beyond what we have so far taken to be relevant. That is, horizons make evident our failure truly to practice emptiness—becoming attentive to the interdependence and mutual relevance of all things.

Practicing Chan is not a spiritual discipline that requires us to retreat into a cave or a remote forest. It is a way of being present that can—and, finally, must—be undertaken in the midst of everyday circumstances. It is not an exercise of single-pointed concentration (the narrow, technical meaning of "*samadhi*") but of illuminating and bringing to full expression the enlightening character and nonduality of all things. This is what Vimalakirti pointed toward with his claim that "in a buddha-realm, all things do the great work of enlightenment. Even shit and piss!" It is what Bodhidharma meant by the principle of confidence in the "one true nature" of all things—their disposition toward a liberating absence of opposition or obstruction.

In Huineng's teaching of the readiness to awaken, there is an utter optimism about our capacity for realizing freedom from suffering, here and now. The exercise of meditative wisdom cannot require elaborate ritual preparations or setting aside specially designated times and places for practice. Given that all things have buddha-nature—the disposition toward liberating relationships—each and every place and moment must be open to awakening just as they are. At the same time, this means that it is not possible to exercise meditative wisdom if we want to do so. If we find ourselves in the position of wanting liberation or awakening, we are already stuck in delusion. If awakening lies somewhere over the horizon of our present situation—in some other time or some other place—then it is nothing more than a figment of one's imagination.

Huineng's teaching thus poses a profound question. If all things in this world realm are doing the work of enlightenment, how is it that you and I remain snared in patterns of chronic suffering and crisis? How is it that we are not yet awakened? If the problem is not the real existence of polluting dusts that obscure our original nature, what is it? Huineng responds in a way that recalls the Daoism of Laozi and Zhuangzi. Our problem lies in habitual and erroneous patterns of relationship and attention. If we can resist falling into and getting stuck in these patterns, nothing further is necessary. We do not need to develop anything new—anything that is not already our own. We only need to refrain from doing the kinds of things that blind us to our own original nature.

Huineng says that, in his teaching lineage, "everyone has established no-thought as the ancestral teaching, no-appearances as the body, and no-dwelling as the root." These are not references to states of affairs we might attain, however, but to ongoing practices. "No-appearances is being among appearances but not caught by them. No-thought is being in the midst of thoughts but not thinking them. No-dwelling is expressing our original nature." Appearances mark our perspective on things. A stepladder seen from the side appears like the letter "A." The same ladder seen from the front appears to be rectangular, with several cross-members between each vertical leg. Seen from a distance, a house may appear stately and grand. Seen up close, it may appear run-down and abandoned. Appearances depend, in other words, on a particular view of things and are necessarily limited. Separating from appearances does not mean closing off our senses and retreating into a purely internal consciousness. Instead, it means attending to things in an unlimited way—being horizonlessly aware. Huineng's practice of no-appearances is "not separating from all things but only from the appearances of things." Reminiscent of the purpose of Bodhidharma's "wall-like gazing," Huineng says that as soon as we have no-appearances, "our nature and body are pure and clear."

Purity and clarity here are not characteristics of one's nature and body but are the absence of any fixed characteristics. Huineng explicitly criticizes the notion that one can purify the mind or clean the environment. In setting up the intention to do so, we already create an impure mind and a dirty environment that must be dissolved, destroyed, and replaced. Far from being a means toward freeing ourselves from duality, this intention perpetuates it. Practicing no-appearances is realizing conditions under which one's body and nature will not be marked by any limiting characteristics or boundaries, exhibiting nothing that could be stained, obscured, or opposed. No-appearances can be seen as the body of Chan practice and the readiness to awaken precisely because it restores the horizonless interdependence and interpenetration of all things. Practicing no-appearances empties our situation of the conditions for existence and dissolves the basis for conflict and suffering.

How can this be done? As long as we are alive, in or as human bodies, how is it possible to realize limitless awareness—awareness untainted by appearances and views? Huineng answers, by not thinking. Like no-appearances, the practice of no-thought does not bring about a lapse into unconsciousness or blank-headed staring. Huineng states that it is simply "in all situations, not being stained." That is, practicing no-thought is the condition of having no-appearances. It is being present in such a way that there are no things that stain and no things being stained. This is not inattentiveness but attentiveness freed from any opposition or resistance. Thoughts take place as always, one passing into another without a rest. But in practicing no-thought, this process occurs without generating the sense of being the thinker of these thoughts. Being unstained in all situations means having no self to which any residue from an experience or action could cling. At the same time, it means not marking anything or any situation as mine or yours.

This opens us to the freedom of nonduality. We stop identifying ourselves as thinkers caught up in and karmically tied down by "this is not acceptable" or "that is desirable," or "nothing really matters." No-thought is realizing what it means to have no fixed location, to be liberated from what is or is not real, relevant, or resisting. The way out of conflict and opposition is not to champion one way over another. It is not to claim this is true and all else is false. The way out—an always available middle path—is through "not dwelling on either objective things or subjective experiences." This is seeing our original or root nature.

This way out should not, however, be confused with simply forgetting all about our pasts and paying no heed to our futures. Not dwelling on things is not undertaken by withdrawing from responsibility for redirecting the meaning of our situation. On the contrary, Huineng makes it clear to his students that they should take the four great vows to liberate all sentient beings, cut off errant passions, study all the Buddhist teachings, and traverse the unsurpassed Buddha way. Chan is a life of unremitting and compassionate engagement. It is also a life of full self-disclosure. We cannot hide past mistakes and wrongdoing behind present holiness. We must, in fact, generate intense awareness of our mistakes and wrongdoings and seek forgiveness for them. But seeking forgiveness means "moment by moment not being stained by ignorance and casting aside bad actions of the past . . . casting aside previous arrogant minds . . . [and] casting aside prior feelings of jealousy." Chan is an utter turning about of those thoughts and actions through which we constructed and maintained the conceit of self-existence. The surest strategy for doing so is to "not make anything." Real repentance for past wrongs is not done with the mouth but by refraining from making good and bad, pure and impure, merit and sin. "Don't just talk about emptiness with your mouth and fail to practice it!" he warns (*Platform Sutra*, section 22). Stop making the path and the goal at its far end. Demonstrate, here and now, your readiness for awakening.

This is not easy to accomplish on our own. Huineng repeatedly tells his students that there is nothing to rely on but their own natures and that Chan practice is not something that can be done for us. It is not something to be appreciated intellectually and left at that. It is something we must do ourselves. But he also insists that this does not mean arrogantly believing we can pull ourselves up by our own bootstraps. He avows that his own teaching has been handed down from generation to generation and is not something he has invented on his own. Although our own nature is originally enlightening, we must still enter into relationship with "a good teacher who will show [us] how to see [our] own nature" (*Platform Sutra*, section 12). Our nature and its revelation in the readiness to awaken is thoroughly and infinitely relational.

Mazu

In the *Platform Sutra*, Huineng's teachings are not presented abstractly. They record "live" interactions between Huineng as spiritual guide and people with whom he has the karma for serving in this capacity. As the Chan tradition develops, "discourse records" of meetings between masters and disciples (and less commonly between two masters) are vested with the highest degree of authority. This is not because the words that they exchange are wonders of literary expression. On the contrary, they evidence a disdain for refined speech and an inclination toward everyday patterns of speaking, simple vocabularies, and a heavy use of local slang and idiom. The profound authority of Chan discourse records lies in the fact that they embody the relational energy of encounters between spiritual masters and their disciples. In them are captured the strikingly unique blossoming of the readiness to awaken.

In this sense, Chan discourse records are very much like Chinese calligraphy—traditionally considered by Chinese to be the most spontaneous and telling form of art. A great work of calligraphy is not a representation of any ideal or literal form. Rather, it employs a particular word or phrase as a medium through which a fleeting course of energy is made manifest and recorded. The finished work resembles, perhaps more than anything else, a recording of a music performance —especially an improvised form of music like jazz as performed before a live audience. Likewise, Chan encounter dialogues record the spirit of a shared improvisation of awakening. Their authoritative and creative quality is not primarily a function of which words are used, in which order, and with which precise connotations. Rather, it is a function of their live feel—their ability to evoke, even here and now, a space of unlimited immediacy.

Extending the analogy with jazz, one might compare the Chan records of Huineng to recordings of music by Duke Ellington or Louis Armstrong. By contrast, the discourse records of Mazu and his dharma heirs would be comparable to the recordings of Miles Davis or John Coltrane. With their radical embrace of unprecedented demonstrations of the relational meaning of the readiness to awaken, Mazu and his heirs stretch language and social propriety to their breaking points. With skilled abandon, they lay utter waste to any notion that Buddhism is quietist, that ritual formalities are essential to its practice, and that the master-disciple relationship is an essentially calming one based on confirming shared contemplative insights.

Mazu is the first Chan master to have used the controversial techniques of shouting, hitting, and "illogical" conversations in working with his students. These "shock tactics" would eventually become a standard part of the Chan master's strategic repertoire, most likely because of their apparent success. One hundred thirty-nine of Mazu's students are said to have developed a profound ability to express Chan awakening—more than any other Chan master on record. With Mazu, the master-disciple relationship moves to center stage, and the demonstration of Chan awakening becomes a duet. As a legacy of this shift, from the ninth century on, collections of the "encounter dialogues" taking place between masters and their disciples come to be seen as the most authoritative expression of the meaning of Chan. By the eleventh century, these dialogues are crafted into collections of "public cases" (Chinese, *gongan;* Japanese, *koan*) and institutionalized as part of the basic curriculum of a Chan education.

Like the shift in jazz sensibilities brought into seminal focus by Miles Davis, the innovations in Chan teaching that were initiated by Mazu were responsive to the needs of a time. In Mazu's case, these responses took place in the aftermath of the An Lushan rebellion and what was surely one of the most tragic decades in Chinese history. There is no doubt that the urgent, no-holds-barred quality of his teaching style arose—at least in part—out of a need to break through the spiritual paralysis afflicting China during the early decades of his teaching career.

Little is known of Mazu's origins. He was born in Sichuan province near the Tibetan border in 709. Before his thirtieth birthday, he studied under two important Chan teachers: Chuji—a second-generation dharma heir of Hongren, the fifth patriarch—and his student Wuxiang. The style of Chan practiced by Chuji and Wuxiang stressed spontaneity, nonduality, and a casual attitude regarding Buddhist meditation techniques, ritual formalities, and precepts. It was a rustic, freewheeling style of Chan that was described by its proponents as "vivid and alive" and by its detractors as "dangerous" in its extreme commitment to nonduality.

Leaving Sichuan for central China, Mazu spent several years engaged in the practice of sitting meditation. A spiritual turning point came during a solo meditation retreat at Chuanfa monastery, where he had a life-changing encounter with the seventh patriarch, Huairang. During this period of Chinese history, it was common for solo and group meditation retreats to last for up to sixty days, with a daily regimen of sixteen to eighteen hours of sitting meditation and perhaps three to four hours of chanting or sutra recitation. One can imagine Mazu in the midst of his retreat, sitting wall-like in silent meditation. He becomes aware of a grating sound from outside his meditation hut but continues to sit quietly focused. As the sound continues and grows louder, however, irritation begins to grow. Every so often, the grating sound turns into a torn screech, like that produced by a piece of chalk scraped across a blackboard. Finally, Mazu has had enough. He unfolds his legs, rises, and steps outside to investigate. He sees Huairang seated in the grass outside the hut, methodically scraping a broken roofing tile against a block of stone.

"What are you doing?" he demands to know, almost surely wondering why this monk would be making such an irritating noise outside his meditation quarters.

Huairang looks up casually and replies, "I'm making a mirror."

"A mirror!" Mazu is incredulous. "You can't make a mirror out of a roofing tile!"

"Oh, really? Well, if I can't make a mirror by polishing a roofing tile, what makes you think you can make yourself into a buddha by sitting in meditation?"

Mazu is clearly taken aback by this. "So what should I do?"

"In this situation, it's like there's an ox yoked to a cart. If the cart isn't moving, do you hit the cart or the ox?"

Mazu isn't quite sure how to answer. Huairang picks up the thread. "Look, you're either training for sitting Chan meditation or you're training for sitting as Buddha. If you're training for sitting Chan meditation, [know that] Chan meditation is not a matter of either sitting or reclining. If you're training to sit as Buddha, [know that] Buddha has no fixed form. According to the teaching of nonabiding, you shouldn't respond [to things] with grasping or rejecting. You, supposedly 'sitting as Buddha,' are just killing Buddha. If you hold onto the sitting form, then that is not penetrating his [naturally fluid] pattern of relating."

Huairang's criticism hits home. Mazu feels as if he has just drunk ambrosia and wants to know what the function of mind is in encompassing this formless *samadhi,* or attentive virtuosity. Huairang dismisses the idea that there is something special that Mazu must undertake to realize what it means to sit as Buddha. His teaching is like a rain that will soak into Mazu's mind-ground and cause the seeds of awakening already sown there to sprout, enabling Mazu to see his path *(dao).*

Mazu is still caught up in being an unenlightened subject with an objective goal of awakening. He wants to know how he will see the path, since it is one of emptiness and has neither color nor form.

Huairang is not taken in by Mazu's cleverness. He responds by saying that "the mind-ground's dharma eye is able to see from the path. The formless *samadhi* is also just like this." Hearing this, Mazu is opened up and awakened, his emotions and thoughts set free.

In this exchange, Mazu is first reprimanded for having an instrumental understanding of meditation—believing that it is a method for arriving at a projected goal of enlightenment or realized buddhanature. Huairang initiates the exchange by "foolishly" rubbing a roofing tile on a stone in an attempt to make a mirror. In China at that time, mirrors were made of highly polished metal, so Huairang's error is not in terms of the motion he's making. His mistake lies in his choice of materials. Likewise, Mazu's error lies in thinking that sitting in a quiet place in a certain posture is the key to awakening to his own nature. His "roofing tile," or mistaken material, is precisely his situation of retreat into a meditation hut. Chan is something to be practiced in all situations and all postures. There is nothing special about sitting. The point is to conduct oneself as a buddha, not to sit in silent contemplation of a way to become an awakened one.

Mazu only partially gets Huairang's point. He asks how he should discipline his mind in order to realize his nature as a buddha and conduct himself accordingly. Huairang replies that the true dharma eye does not see the path as an object. Rather, it sees from the path. Since the path is that of uninterrupted interdependence and emptiness, the mark of awakening is simply unlimited or horizonless presence. The path is our situation as it is, directed toward liberation, not suffering.

Following his opening, Mazu did not leave Huairang's company but continued deepening his practice—his capacity for responsive virtuosity—under his master's guidance for ten years. He departed sometime around 750 C.E. and only surfaced again in the late 770s. During the decades he was on the road, China's population was cut from 53 to 17 million people by the effects of rebellion, social unrest, border clashes, and famine. When Mazu took up permanent residence at Kaiyuan monastery, there is little doubt that his teaching methods reflected what he had witnessed traveling through China in crisis.

It is hard to imagine the spiritual distress of people who have seen two out of every three friends and relatives die or disappear over a single nine-year period. The unrelenting onslaught of tragedy would, under any circumstances, drive the surviving population to its emotional and communal limits. But in China, the effects of such widespread calamity would have been greatly magnified. For a thousand years, Chinese had associated communal prosperity and social harmony with *tianming,* or the "celestial mandate." Any persistent natural disasters, periods of social unrest, or famine were perceived as evidence that the celestial mandate had been withdrawn or broken—that human society and government had fallen out of accord with the cosmic Dao. Historically, the persistence of disharmony was seen as warrant to challenge existing authorities—political, in particular, but also religious and cultural. The relentless collapse of Chinese society from 755 to 764 would have thrown all authorities into question.

First and foremost would have been the Tang court and its ritual and intellectual foundations. But it would also have thrown into question the authority of Chinese Buddhism. In particular, powerful doubts would have been cast on the forms practiced by elite society and the royal court. But popular understandings of karma would also have forced people to reflect on their own responsibility for the tragedies afflicting their families and communities. As it became clear how widespread the disasters befalling China really were, it would have been impossible not to ask whether China had forsaken the true Dharma and begun sliding into spiritual abyss.

The teachings of Mazu have the radical immediacy of relationships forged in the midst of crisis intervention and emergency. At their core is a call to author a renewal of the true spirit of Buddhist practice. Direct and situation-specific, this was not a generic appeal for reform. It was a personal challenge of the most imperative and yet compassionate sort.

Mazu's recorded lectures begin by sounding a clear call to unreserved presence: "Each and every one of you, be confident that your own mind is Buddha. This mind right now is Buddha." Against the backdrop of China's most tragic decade, this call to the present is no casual invitation to stop holding onto the past and anticipating the future. It is a spiritual battle cry aimed at waking a population in shock—a population all too ready to give in to moral exhaustion and to give up any hope of making a meaningful difference. For many, this would have meant blindly fleeing into either utterly selfish opportunism or transcendently mystical abstraction. Mazu's claim that "everyday mind is Buddha" effectively cuts off both escape routes. The Middle Path and its infinite resources for turning things toward liberation can be traveled right here, right now.

Huineng said that seeing into our own nature is like "the great ocean gathering all the flowing streams, merging together all the waters small and great into one." Our own nature is a nexus of flows of energy, a coming together of infinite individual karmic streams of intention and value. Mazu refers to realizing this nexus as the "ocean seal *samadhi*"—"taking in all things, it's like one hundred thousand streams equally returning to the great ocean." For Mazu, it means actively opening up to all things at all times. It is not some kind of sacred ritual to be practiced only on rare occasions by the spiritually elect. It is not something for which we must undergo extensive training. "The Dao is not a function of cultivation. . . . If you want to understand your path *(dao),* [realize that] ordinary mind is the Dao. . . . Just like right now, whether walking, standing, sitting, or lying down, responding to opportunity/danger and joining things is entirely the Dao."

Seeing matters in this way is not the way of the commoner or the sage. It is, according to Mazu, the practice of the bodhisattva. It is a practice of establishing a compassionately clear direction for the meaning of our entire, present situation. "Joining things" is the horizonless way *(dao)* of healing the wound of existence. We embark on the Way (Dao) by "refraining from making anything"—resisting the temptation to make good and bad, saint and sinner, nirvana and samsara. Making such distinctions only creates and further cements barriers between things. Doing so intentionally is to make karma for living within barricades, and a barricaded life is, finally, an increasingly impoverished one. Cut off from the contributions of others, we consume ourselves in endless wanting and resisting. Bodhisattva practice means seeing that, "all dharmas are buddha-dharmas; all dharmas are liberating."

Because the term "dharma" can mean both things or beings in general as well as teachings, Mazu is not only repeating Vimalakirti's claim that all things are doing the work of enlightenment. He is insisting that all things and beings are teaching. Unlike the words and letters copied into books and circulated as sacred texts, these teachings are the "live words" of the Buddha—his preaching in and for this present moment. Given this, what could we possibly be lacking? What could we need to resist? What could we possibly seek?

Mazu challenges his students not only to follow Bodhidharma's practice of accepting the karma of their present situation, but also to take it up and actively transform things with the energy it focuses. "At all times and in all places, bring about a buddha!" He is explicit about what this means. "A buddha is capable of authoritative personhood *(ren)*. Having realized understanding kindness and the excellent nature of opportunities and dangers, one is able to break through the net of doubts snaring all sentient beings. Departing from is, is-not, and other such bondages . . . leaping over quantity and calculation, one is without obstruction in whatever one does. When your situation and its pattern are both penetrated, [your actions] are like the sky giving rise to clouds: suddenly they exist and then they don't. Not leaving behind any obstructing traces, they are like phrases written with water."

Mazu's imagery perfectly captures his point. Don't leave any lasting mark or signature on the world. Simply offer, moment by moment, what will open your situation to meaning the liberation of all beings. The conduct of bodhisattvas strikes a middle way between the Confucian ideal of action based on clear, historical precedents and the Daoist ideal of nonaction based on a return to naturalness. It is conduct that is uncalculated, arising without premeditation or preconditions. And yet it is conduct that serves its function without remainder. The bodhisattva's work is such that when it is done, no one remains—neither sentient beings who have been saved nor enlightening beings who have accomplished their saving. For this work, there can be no training, no trial runs, and no game plans.

The spiritual courage that this requires is immense. It is a courage that can only be rooted in limitless confidence or faith in one own nature. If this kind of authoritative and compassionate nature is to be realized, no gap can be permitted in exercising attentive virtuosity and the readiness to awaken. Any hesitation, any thought given to what must be done and why, is already to have fallen into the duality of what is or is not appropriate, what will or will not work.

Mazu's experience practicing under iconoclastic and freewheeling Chan masters in his native Sichuan would have made him well aware of the dangers of advocating radical spontaneity. Too often, being spontaneous is just another way of saying "unconsciously acting out one's karma"—a way of warranting already existing habits and dispositions. Virtuosity is not just immediately reacting but truly and compassionately responding. The shock tactics for which Mazu became famous were undoubtedly developed, in part, to cut through the self-centered illusion of acting spontaneously and being free. But they would also have served to demonstrate stunningly the naked and virtuosic immediacy of living without precedents, customs, and habits. Given his inheritance of Huineng's teaching of the need for awakening "with this very body," it is no wonder that many of Mazu's most incisive "shocks" were arrestingly physical in nature.

Once, a student in the assembly asked about the meaning of Bodhidharma coming from the West. Mazu motioned the student forward, saying, "Come closer, I want to answer you privately." As the student walked up and came to stop before him, Mazu leaned forward as if to whisper something and then suddenly boxed the student's ears. "Six ears [the student's, Bodhidharma's, and Mazu's] don't plot together. Come back tomorrow." The student returned the following day and asked Mazu to instruct him. Mazu scolded him. "Just go away. Wait until I've gone into the dharma hall. When I'm about to talk, come forward and I'll give you some proof." With this, the student awakened.

To another student asking the meaning of Bodhidharma coming to China, Mazu requested that he demonstrate how to bow. As the student bent over, Mazu kicked him. The student collapsed onto the ground with a great awakening. He got up, clapping his hands, and let out a great belly laugh. "How wonderful! How wonderful! The root of a hundred thousand *samadhis* and incalculable subtle meanings can be realized at the tip of a single hair!" Later he told the assembly, "From the moment I was subjected to Mazu's kick right on up to the present, my laughter hasn't stopped."

Another student was rolling a wheelbarrow of dirt alongside the dharma hall when he came across Mazu seated, leaning against the wall with his legs stretched out in the sun. The student asked him to please move his legs. "As I've already stretched them out, I'm not going to move them away," Mazu replied. The student retorted, "Well, then, given that I'm already rolling down this path, I'm not going to turn around." He rolled over Mazu's legs. Mazu's legs were badly bruised, and he went behind the dharma hall, grabbed an ax, and came out yelling, "Whoever just came from rolling over this old monk's legs, come out!" The student came forward and stretched out his neck. Mazu smiled and put away the ax.

Such stories and many others like them reveal Mazu's community as one of great trust and commitment, but also great humor and refreshing informality. The number of students that Mazu guided to awakening in just ten years of teaching is a testament to his masterful practice of skillful means and his powerfully creative imagination. For Mazu, Chan meant taking whatever is given and using it to flip the meaning of the situation toward awakening. Crucial to his ability to do this was his freedom to take whatever position was needed to get the necessary leverage.

A monk once asked him why he taught "present mind is Buddha." Mazu said, "To stop the crying of small children."

The monk wanted to know, "When the crying stops, what then?" Mazu replied, "Not mind, not Buddha."

"So, if someone comes along who has gone beyond these two kinds of expedients, what will you point to as the ancestral doctrine then?"

"Then I'd tell him, 'Not being anything.'"

Still the monk persisted. "What if you meet someone who comes from the Middle Path?"

Mazu said, "Then I would teach him to join bodily and communicate the great Dao."

The sequence of Mazu's replies illustrates that there is no one size fits all approach to liberating beings from suffering, no universal message or method. Any response to opportunity must take place from the midst of a situation, not from the outside in keeping with some fixed set of precedents. At the same time, however, the sequence also suggests three interwoven strands of directed movement: first, from affirmation through negation to shared realization; second, from the familiar and certain through the openly unknown and uncertain to demonstrating focused and yet limitless coherence; and, finally, from dependence on conditions through both partial and entire independence from conditions to a fully harmonizing interdependence.

All three movements converge on the body. Mazu claims that the world's myriad things and beings should be seen as "one's own family." We are all, in some way, related. Indeed, the emptiness and interdependence of all things can be seen as another way of saying that the wondrous functioning of the myriad things "all are one's own body." The body is not a thing standing alone and apart from countless other things in a world that contains all with utter dispassion. It is a distillation of the pattern of all things, a unique and expressive gathering of our entire situation. Simultaneously, the body is an opening onto and an opening up of our situation. Thus, Mazu points out that since all things express the single heart-mind of our shared buddha-nature, when "one is awakened, ten thousand follow." The culmination of Mazu's approach to Chan is thus definitely not a transcendent leap from our present situation into heavenly otherness. It consists of an utterly flexible "harmony of body and mind that reaches out through all four limbs . . . benefiting what can't be benefited and doing what can't be done."

At bottom, realizing this harmony means conducting ourselves as buddhas and bodhisattvas right here and right now, in the midst of our present relationships, just as they have come to be. Although this is perhaps easiest for those who have left the home life and taken ordination, as proven by Mazu's famous student, Layman Pang—a free-thinking poet known throughout China—it is possible even for those remaining with spouse and children. Indeed, as Layman Pang demonstrated, it is even possible for Chan to be practiced with one's family. Chan is not a matter of sitting in meditation in order to become awakened but of carrying out every action from walking to sitting to standing or lying down in unflinching readiness to awaken. In doing so, we cannot lapse either into denials of what is occurring here and now or into longing for what has not yet come to be. Instead, we must with uncompromising attentiveness make use of precisely the resources present to revise the meaning of our situation—whatever it may be—from one of blockage and bondage to limitlessly fluent liberation.

Linji

The creative tension between the need for limitless intimacy with our situation and the need for improvisational virtuosity were crucial to the texture of Chan life in ninth-century China. In practice, its resolution fostered the emergence of a wide (and often wild) array of characters demonstrating virtually indomitable responsive clarity. Trained to develop freedom from reliance on written scriptures, profound attentive virtuosity, and unwavering readiness to respond to the shifting needs of the moment, Chan practitioners were well poised to weather the great purge of Buddhism ordered by Emperor Wuzong from 842 to 845 C.E. In this short period, roughly five thousand temples and forty thousand shrines were destroyed, and nearly a quarter of a million monks and nuns were forced back into lay life. Because the purge involved the devastation of most large Buddhist libraries, the text-based Chinese schools suffered most, effectively disappearing until their approaches to Buddhism were reintroduced from Korea in the Song dynasty. When the emperor died and Buddhism's imperial sanction was officially reinstated, Chan emerged as its leading form of practice.

Sometime in the late 830s, a young monk arrived at Huangbo's monastery. Well versed in the sutras and commentaries, trained in meditation, and a devoted follower of monastic discipline, Linji eventually attracted the attention of one of Huangbo's monks. He was referred to the master himself for a private interview. Linji entered the master's quarters, bowed, and began to ask the question he had been instructed to pose: What is the cardinal principle of the buddhadharma? Before he could finish, Huangbo struck him with his Chan staff and drove him from the room. After consulting with the monk who had arranged the interview, Linji returned twice more with the same question and the same result.

Dejected and determined to leave the monastery, Linji apologized to the monk. "Lucky for me, you were compassionate enough to send me to question the master. Three times I raised the question and three times I received blows. I regret that because of some karmic blockage I can't get the point of his profound instruction. For now, I'm going to pull out and go." The monk insisted that he report to Huangbo before leaving and then spoke directly with the master on Linji's behalf. When Linji arrived, Huangbo said that if he intended to leave, he should only go to the place of an associate of his, Dayu.

Linji did as instructed and soon found himself explaining his encounters with Huangbo to Dayu, admitting that he didn't know where his error lay. When he finished, Dayu shook his head in dismay. "Huangbo, like an old grandmother, succeeded in exhausting himself on your behalf. And you still have the nerve to come here asking where you went wrong!"

With this, Linji attained a great awakening. "Hah!" he exclaimed, "so there really isn't much to Huangbo's buddha-dharma!"

Dayu throttled Linji and shook him. "You bed-wetting little imp! You came here asking where you had gone wrong and now you're announcing that there's nothing special about Huangbo's teaching. Tell me what principle of the Way you've seen! Speak! Speak!"

Linji gave Dayu three quick jabs to the ribs. Dayu let go of him and said, "Your master is Huangbo. This isn't any of my business."

Linji returned to Huangbo's monastery, where he was immediately treated to a derisive greeting. "This guy again? Coming and going, coming and going . . . when is this going to end?"

"It's all because of your grandmotherly kindness," Linji replied, presenting a customary gift. Huangbo set the gift aside and asked what had happened at Dayu's place. Linji related his encounter. When he finished, Huangbo said, "How I'd love to get a hold of this fellow. I'm aching to give him a taste of my stick."

"Why say you're waiting?" Linji asked. "Eat right now!" With this, he slapped Huangbo.

Huangbo exclaimed, "What a lunatic! Coming here to pull the tiger's whiskers."

Linji roared.

After his initial awakening, Linji—like Mazu before him—practiced under his master's guidance for nearly ten more years. At least several of these, most likely the years of Wuzong's purge of Buddhism, he spent living at Chan master Dayu's remote hermitage. Around 850, he went on the road for several years, traveled throughout China visiting sacred sites of Chan, and eventually settled in the north, where he taught for roughly ten years until his death. Over time, the keen-eyed strength of his character and his fiercely direct expression of Chan would assume legendary status.

The respect given to Linji reveals a great deal about the Chinese context of Chan's evolution from Bodhidharma, sitting in a cave by himself in the practice of wall-like gazing, to Linji, going toe-to-toe with Chan's leading torchbearers. The key to understanding Linji's peerless authority as a Chan exemplar lies in reconciling the apparent contradictions present in the account of his awakening. Buddhism is renowned as a tradition espousing nonviolence, equanimity, and compassion. How is it that Linji's awakening came as the result of reflecting on being beaten with a two-inch-thick wooden staff? How can it be that his awakening was confirmed when he treated his teachers to punches and slaps?

Huangbo's teacher, Baizhang, once said, "Those whose insight is the same as their teachers' lack half their teachers' power. Only someone whose insight surpasses his or her teacher's is worthy to be the teacher's heir." When he first approaches Huangbo, Linji is not even allowed to finish his question before he is struck. He is not allowed, in other words, to settle himself into position as an ignorant student seeking insight from one who knows. By the end of his third visit, Linji is completely frustrated and despairing. Not seeing Huangbo's true intentions, he feels that he has proven himself to be unworthy of instruction. Believing himself to be a victim of his own karma, he decides to leave Huangbo's monastery like a dog with his tail between his legs.

Instead, he ends up being sent to Dayu, whose remarks about Huangbo's grandmotherly exhaustion bring about a gestalt shift in Linji's view of things. He suddenly sees that the blows were not intended to prove his unworthiness but to prevent him from stating —and effectively establishing—his own lack of worth. In other words, Huangbo's blows were preventative medicine. Linji is freed by this realization. Huangbo really had nothing to teach after all, and he himself had nothing to learn. Dayu sees the light go on in Linji's expression, grabs him by the throat, and demands that he confess what he's realized.

Linji is not taken in by the ploy—an invitation to try saying what enlightenment is—and demonstrates his insight instead. Three quick punches and Dayu releases him. Doing so, both are freed from grappling. Linji proves he cannot be caught by his situation. Upon returning to Huangbo, Linji is not deterred by his teacher's dismissive remarks. Instead, he greets Huangbo with an offering or gift. Huangbo asks for more: an account of what happened with Dayu. When Huangbo caps Linji's story by announcing his desire to deliver a good taste of his stick—more grandmotherly kindness—Linji beats him to the punch. He verbally hits Huangbo for hesitating. Asking his teacher why he's falling into the trap of wanting and waiting, Linji gives him the taste that he's been aching for: a medicinal slap to wake him up. With this, Linji demonstrates that he has what it will take to surpass Huangbo.

The themes brought into focus by Linji's enlightenment narrative are woven throughout his own teachings. The record of his discourses begins with him being asked by the provincial governor to take the high seat at the front of the dharma hall and deliver a teaching about the meaning of Buddhist awakening. Linji admits that he cannot refuse the governor's invitation. Nevertheless, "as soon as I open my mouth, I'll have made a mistake." According to the tradition of the Chan patriarchs, the great matter of liberation is not something addressed through speech. Still, Linji allows that if he says nothing at all, then the monks and laypeople gathered in the dharma hall will have nowhere to place their feet, nothing to push off against and leap into demonstrated readiness to awaken. Refusing to teach would be like presenting a fishing net as a gift but not the drawstring that enables it to be cast and pulled closed.

But instead of offering doctrines and explanations, Linji's practice was to challenge his audience, asking if any among them would be ready to enter into "dharma combat." In a typical occurrence, a monk came forward before the assembly and asked Linji to explain the meaning of one of his teaching phrases: the "true person of no rank."

In response, Linji leapt down off the teaching platform, took the monk by the throat, and began choking him, demanding that he "speak! speak!" Unlike Linji in his encounter with Dayu, the monk hesitates, deliberating about what to do. He is turned loose with a snort and a crude rebuke. "What kind of used shit-wiping stick is this 'true person of no rank'?" Linji wants to know.

By hesitating, the monk demonstrates that his readiness to awaken still has limits. By jumping down unexpectedly and taking the monk by the throat, Linji takes on the role of the highway robber bent on stealing the monk's treasure—his true nature. Instead of treating him as such, however, the monk freezes. Most likely, he has planned out his course of action well in advance, having witnessed many episodes of dharma combat and having seen what he has believed is an opening. But, caught in front of the assembly, with his master's thumbs pressing his windpipe closed, and being shouted at to speak, he is at least momentarily at a loss.

Disappointed, Linji pushes him away with an utterly derisive remark. If this "student" is not even able to handle the grandmotherly toughness of his master, how could he even imagine being able to handle the blind and covetous violence of a real thief? How could he hope to respond in an enlightening fashion to the grief of an orphan, or the white-hot rage of a father whose daughter has been raped, or to the numbingly cold calculations of an emperor bent on destroying the Dharma? A true person of no rank is someone who has no fixed position to act from, no fixed principles according to which courses of action must be undertaken, no set formulas for calculating utility.

Only a person unburdened by such limitations is able to respond immediately and as needed in any situation whatsoever.

Importantly, only a true person of no rank is able to free others from their own fixed identities. As long as the monk is hung up on being just a student, Linji is forced into the mold of teacher. In the context of a society largely organized along Confucian lines, it is imperative to know one's place or rank within a situation and to act accordingly. It is not the place of a student to correct a teacher or that of a peasant to govern an aristocrat. The duties and responsibilities of each and every person in a situation are, at least ideally, prescribed. Linji's understanding of the meaning of bodhisattva action is that there are ultimately no horizons for our responsibility and thus no limits to the kinds of conduct into which we will find ourselves drawn in carrying out the work of awakening all beings. We must be ready to shift perspectives as needed without depending on anything.

True persons of no rank are as "lively as fish jumping in the water and simply perform their function in response to all situations." As Linji's teacher put it, "In responding without having any fixed perspective, you are bringing forth your heart ... [and] this is known as 'supreme enlightenment.'" In conducting ourselves as true persons of no rank, there is no room for either hesitation or doubts.

"Students of the Way nowadays aren't getting anywhere," Linji laments.

> What's your problem? Simply put: not believing in yourselves. If you don't attain complete confidence in yourselves, you'll keep bumbling along, following any kind of circumstances in utter bewilderment. You'll suffer through repeated immersion in changing circumstances and will never attain freedom.... Do you want to discern the patriarchs and buddhas? They are just you who stand before me listening to my ancestral teaching. But since you haven't realized true confidence in yourselves, you face outward running around in search. Even if your seeking is successful, you'll only end up with the victorious forms of cultural precedents and written words and never the living spirit of the patriarchs.

Linji dismisses the idea that students of the Buddhist path are to place their faith or confidence in the sutras or commentaries. "Bud-

dha" and "nirvana" are nothing more than "hitching posts for donkeys." There is no need to go into deep theories and laborious studies.
In phrases that recall Zhuangzi's rebuttal of Confucian concerns for
proper ritual activity and reliance on authorities of the past, Linji
claims that "the buddha-dharma is not hard work. Just be ordinary
and have no worries. I shit, piss, put on clothes, eat food, and when
fatigue sets in, I lie down. Foolish people laugh at me. The wise, however, understand." In an effort finally to dismiss the idea that there is
something out there to seek, he tells his students that if they should
happen to come across the "Buddha" on the road, they should kill
him.

Linji's Chan involves a radical denial of any goals to work toward
and an equally radical embrace of our own situation and its limitless
possibilities for awakening. The true person of no rank is a slap in the
face of Confucian propriety. But Linji is not a Daoist going along with
the natural flow of things. He is the heir of Mazu's injunction to "benefit what cannot be benefited and do what cannot be done." Thus, he
insists that we make no mistake about the truly correct understanding
of liberation. "Face the world and walk crosswise," he advises. Take
what is given by the karma focused in the present moment and revise
it. Turn things around. Change their meaning. The responsibility that
goes along with taking the bodhisattva vows of Mahayana Buddhism
does not have any limit. And the only way to shoulder it is to be
unburdened by any habits or doubts. The task is to make yourself the
master of any situation. Doing so, everywhere you stand is real—the
bodhimandala, or place of awakening. Doing so, "even though circumstances come and go, they won't be able to influence or catch
you. Even if in previous lives you had the bad habit of making the five
gateless karmas, by themselves they become the great ocean of
liberation."

For Linji, this mastery is not something wielded over and against
our situation. It is something that appears by itself. If hesitation and
doubt spell doom in dharma combat, so does becoming an agent who
acts in a situation. True mastery occurs only in realizing effortless and
horizonless nonduality. It is not a function of willpower or an ability to
command others into action. Willpower and controlling others prove
that we continue to exist in a world that is fundamentally resistant—

a world against which we must push with as much might as we can. Doing so does not prove our liberation or freedom but our arrogance.

In classical Chinese, the term for arrogance literally means "adding on slowness" or "retarding a situation." It points toward the effect of exercising self-centered control over our circumstances—in common slang, being a drag. Enforcing one's own view of things requires a great expenditure of energy. It diverts energy that would normally be circulating throughout our situation, promoting the health of all things. Controlling one's situation means impoverishing it, making it into a situation in which the ten thousand things do not take care of themselves. Instead, they will require constant care and attention. By asserting independence, we force other things and beings either into dependence on us or into conflict with us.

If, however, we are able to realize true nonduality or one-mind, then, as Huangbo puts it, "wriggling beings and all the buddhas and bodhisattvas are a single body and do not differ." The effortlessness that Linji so strongly associates with becoming the master of any situation is like the effortlessness with which we raise a hand in greeting a friend or with which we lift our feet in strolling home through the soft light of dusk. When all things are united as one single body with freely circulating energy, or *qi*, there is no need for willpower. Living cut off from other beings as free agents in a particular situation is like inhabiting a body that has been partially paralyzed. The legs are still present, but they will move only if we consciously take them in our hands and forcibly change their position. It is only when there is an interruption or blockage in the free flow of energy in our situation that force is necessary in order to revise its meaning—the direction and quality of its movement from present to future.

Linji encourages his students to exit from the two-pronged trap of subjectivity and objectivity, the apparent need for willpower, and the association of freedom with control. "Do not be deceived," he insists. "If you turn to the objective, there is no Dharma. Neither is there anything to be achieved by turning to the subjective." The most consistent clue he offers about how to avoid either wrong turn and to realize the mastery that comes with nonduality is to "perceive, right now, who is listening to this teaching. Without form, or marks, or roots, or origin, this one has no abiding status. Flexible and lively . . . the place from which such a one functions is no place at all."

Linji is doing his best here to use language to point toward that which has no location. He is inviting us to stop thinking that enlightenment is something that occurs either here or there, that sometimes is and sometimes is not taking place. If he were to ask his students to realize who is seeing him teach, it would encourage thinking in subjective terms that insist on the possibility of being blocked. Our line of sight, after all, can always be obstructed. Instead, he asks them to attend to the one who is "present right before you, listening to this teaching." Unlike vision, hearing is not directionally focused. We hear what is happening all around us. Moreover, while our view can be blocked, our ability to listen remains open so long as we can hear at all. Whether we sit to the left or right of Linji, at the front of the hall or behind the tallest people in the audience, we can still listen to the teachings. And we do not receive only a partial view of Linji as he speaks—broken glimpses from the side or the front, for example. We listen to the entire room at once, with all the sounds blending without any obstruction.

Linji makes it very clear that while this wide-open nature of listening is important, we should not fall into thinking that the listening he refers to is being carried out by any kind of subject. The one who is listening to the teachings does so from "no place at all"—that is, not from within our bodies or from within any other body, but situationally. While at any given time only some people in the audience are able to see Linji teaching, everyone present is listening. The true person of no rank who is freely functioning before us is nothing other than the realization of unimpeded presence together.

Linji is thus bitingly derisive in his criticism of "shave-headed [monks] who have stuffed themselves with food and then sit down to meditate and practice contemplation, seeking to stop the flow of thoughts, hating noise and seeking out silence." If our buddha-nature is not something to be sought outside, neither is it something to be found inside. When we sit in meditation, Linji urges us to "just sit"— that is, to not make anything. When we act, he urges us to "just act." This is conducting ourselves *wuwei,* or without precedents or goals, without setting up objectives for how things are supposed to turn out as a result of our agency.

Linji claims at one point that there "is no Buddha, no Dharma, no training, and no realization." With characteristic directness, he says that undertaking training to be exemplary bodhisattvas is just another form of making karma. But as he also indicates that the true person of no rank is able to make use of karma in all situations, we should not assume that there is no place in Linji's Chan for disciplined training and practice. As in the case of each of the Chan patriarchs before him, Linji's awakening was followed by years of continued training under his spiritual master.

The meaning of such training can be inferred from Mazu's answer to a student who takes quite seriously the Chan denial that words and letters can convey enlightenment and who, therefore, does not want to read sutras. "However that may be," Mazu advises, "you should do so in the future for the sake of other people." As Linji insists, training is not crucial for awakening; but as his own master, Huangbo, stated, it may well be crucial for "accommodating and guiding" others. If awakening is like freeing our (one true) body from paralysis, continued practice and training serve to transform its natural functioning into the sheer, unhindered virtuosity of a gravity-defying Olympic gymnast or a creativity-inspiring master artist.

In the case of the true person of no rank, however, this virtuosity consists of discerning and opening the gates of wisdom, attentive virtuosity, and moral clarity in any situation whatsoever. Chan mastery is not a once-and-for-all achievement but an ongoing performance of the meaning of unimpeded interdependence—actively demonstrating the Middle Way.

Demonstrating Chan Mastery as a Liberating Quality of Relationship

Huineng said, "It is precisely Buddhist practice/conduct that is Buddha." In attempting to understand this claim, it is important to keep in mind that, traditionally, the first step in formally practicing Buddhism was the ritual of taking refuge in the Three Jewels of the Buddha, the Dharma, and the Sangha—that is, the teacher, the teachings, and the community that arises through them. If Siddhartha Gautama had elected to depart from the earthly cycle of birth and death without demonstrating his own unlimited readiness for awakening (others), there would have been no teachings, no community of men and women engaged in realizing liberation from suffering, and no Buddhist practice. That is, if he had not embarked on his teaching career, there would have been no Buddha—only a fully (but privately) realized Siddhartha Guatama. To say that Chan Buddhist practice or conduct is Buddha is to say that Chan consists of shared awakening through realizing liberating relationships.

By identifying the Buddha with Buddhist practice, Huineng is also subtly alerting us to the fact that, like the Buddha himself, Chan practice is not something made up of bits and pieces. Although we can talk about the Buddha's arms, legs, torso, and head, he is not made up out of these parts. Although we can talk about the three relinquishings, meditation, energy work and so on, Chan practice is not cobbled together out of these parts. Arms, legs, torsos, and heads do not exist and grow on their own that we might combine them to form a human body. Just as our bodies grow all over and all at once, Chan practice grows as the situational expression of our own original buddhanature.

When Chinese Buddhists first began working out what it meant to embark on the Mahayana path of liberating all sentient beings from suffering, the teaching of buddha-nature was crucial. By insisting on unflinching commitment to nonduality, it explained how it was possible to "do what cannot be done and benefit what cannot be benefited"—in the words of the *Diamond Sutra*—how it is possible to travel the infinite length of the bodhisattva path, saving innumerable sentient beings even though no beings are finally saved. To support their conception of buddha-nature as the original nature of all things, Chinese Buddhists turned to the Indian concept of the *tathagatagarbha*, or the "womb/embryo of suchness." As they interpreted this term, it announced that the enlightening qualities of a buddha are nascent in all beings. All that is required to activate this original nature is to give birth to it in practice.

These ideas were extremely important in the advent of Chan and its advocacy of homegrown buddhas. But it quickly became apparent that awakening the embryonic buddha that is our own original nature must be followed with careful nurturing and mentoring. From the moment of conception, the embryo of a child is kept safely nurtured in the mother's womb. After birth, the child is nurtured into maturity in the womb of the family. Likewise, the embryonic buddha that is activated when a student encounters the Dharma or Buddhist teaching must be carefully nurtured if it is to grow to maturity.

The relationship between Chan teacher and Chan student can be described metaphorically as a spiritual marriage that, if profound enough, will lead to the birth of no-self: the realization, in and through relationship, of buddha-nature. If the "marriage" prospers and the embryonic buddha is properly nurtured, there comes a continuous maturation of horizonless presence—the relational demonstration of truly liberating intimacy. This is what Mazu referred to as the "wondrous functioning" of one mind.

It is in the context of such an understanding of the maturation of practice that Huangbo unambiguously states the pivotal step of Chan. "If there's no encounter with a brilliant master who has gone 'beyond the world,' the medicine of the Mahayana will have been swallowed in vain." It is for this reason that such exemplary Chan teachers as Mazu and Linji spent years attending their spiritual master after realizing their own readiness to awaken. Reading the scriptures and discourse records, diligently undertaking meditation, and making appropriate offerings are good. But they are no substitute for the direct encounter with and nurturing by a living exemplar of unlimited compassion and skill in means. It is only in intimate partnership with a master that we can fully participate in "doing what cannot be done and benefiting what cannot be benefited." It is only through such a sustained relationship that we can mature to the point of "going on spontaneously."

It might be thought that this process of maturation could be watched from the outside and its lessons gleaned secondhand. Chan's own insistence that it is a "mind-to-mind transmission beyond cultural precedents and words" is, in part, intended to emphasize precisely the impossibility of any form of distance learning. As an expression of the nonduality of buddha-nature, Chan practice cannot be objectified. We cannot be shown how to do it. Even if we were to watch people engaged in it, they would appear to be doing not much of anything.

According to Huangbo, we must enter into relationship with a master who has gone "beyond the world." Masters are not bound by conventions, by expectations, by wants, or by attachments. They have gone beyond the world in the sense that they are not caught by anything. Although they can freely attend to things as needed, their attention is never literally captured. This is not because they refrain from engaging the trials and tribulations of the world but because they avoid dramatic captivity by continuously offering their attention in virtuosic revisions of the meaning of things. What is already offered cannot be demanded or taken away.

By entering into intimate partnership with such a master, Chan disciples grow out of their initially embryonic capacity for expressing their own buddha-nature. A profound resonance is established through which the disciple's own moral clarity becomes firmly established. With the full maturation of practice, a disciple is given the responsibility of establishing a new generation of the Chan dharma family.

As demonstrated by the lives of the four masters rehearsed here, the practice of Chan spirituality is the realization of appreciative and contributory virtuosity. As the next chapter will illustrate more fully, the system of Chan practice as a whole includes relinquishing our horizons for relevance, responsibility, and readiness and undertaking sustained energy work. But at the heart of Chan practice is the unprecedented realization of dramatic partnership with a clear master. Regardless of the factual or historical status of the traditional Chan lineage, its spiritual meaning is clear and uncontested: passing all at once through the three gates of wisdom, attentive virtuosity, and moral clarity, profoundly expressing the emptiness of all things through the dramatic medium of truly liberating relationships.

CHAPTER 6

Chan Practice as Philosophy and Spirituality

Especially as revealed in the teachings of Bodhidharma, Huineng, Mazu, and Linji, Chan Buddhist spirituality grows out of a profoundly embodied capacity for according with our situation and responding as needed. Although this might seem easy enough, it is not. While Chan Buddhists openly resisted distinguishing between "commoners" and "sages," Chan was generally considered a path of great rigor and unflinching commitment. To begin with, there can be no formula or fixed principles for improvisational virtuosity. Because our situation is always changing, according with it is by nature always a work in progress. Not only that, because our situation is irreducibly karmic, responding as needed must necessarily involve questioning and revising our own intentions and values. According with our situation and responding as needed is never just a matter of "going with the flow," much less one of holding previously fixed goals firmly in sight.

All of this makes it very hard to describe how Chan looks on the ground. If practicing Chan means having no fixed position and doing nothing special, how can one tell whether someone is practicing Chan or simply living the unexceptional life of a slacker? A story from the oral tradition of Korean Chan (Son) suggests that others have felt compelled to ask the same question. As the story goes, a senior student at a large and vibrant rural monastery develops serious doubts about his master's authenticity. As far as he can tell, the master's practice of Chan amounts to nothing more than eating well, strolling in the monastic grounds and nearby mountains and villages, watching the sunset each evening, and reading what the senior monk suspects is poetry and popular literature.

"What do you do that makes you master here?" he finally asks. The master raises his eyebrows, shrugs his shoulders, and smiles sheepishly. "I guess not much of anything. How about you?" The senior monk leaves, greatly annoyed, and with an even greater ball of doubt about his master twisting in his gut. A week later, he is called into the master's quarters. The master is going away on a monthlong journey and wants to entrust the monastery to his senior student. The monk happily accepts the honor and promises to keep everything running smoothly and the two hundred monks practicing diligently.

When the master returns a month later, there are only a dozen monks and a handful of novices remaining. The senior monk relates how frictions heated up from the moment the master left and how, within days, there were open arguments and bickering. In spite of his efforts to smooth things over and exercise authority, things only went from bad to worse. In the end, only those too sick, slow-witted, or young to run off had not deserted the monastery. The master looked about, shrugged, and smiled sheepishly. "I guess it's time to start doing 'not much of anything' again!"

Like this master, Mazu's first teachers in Sichuan were repeatedly and strongly accused of being religious "slackers" who were so committed to nonduality and doing nothing special that they were perceived as threats to social order. Huineng urged his monastic and lay students to take the "precepts of formlessness" and to practice the "formless repentance," insisting that Chan did not have to do with any particular bodily posture or mental state but with having complete confidence in one's own true nature and demonstrating one's capacity for conduct without precedent. Linji himself admitted that his approach to Chan left many people clucking their tongues and thinking him a simpleton or a fool. Apparently, the distinctive character of Chan practice does not rest on any norms or standards of bodily comportment.

But neither does it rest on the achievement of some "internal" state of affairs, the attainment of particular, subjectively experienced altered states and supernatural powers, or the realization of intellectual or rhetorical brilliance. Mazu is adamant that "talk about attainment is your mind. Talk about nonattainment is still your mind. Even if you were to get as far as splitting the body, emanating light, and manifesting the eighteen subtle transformations . . . [or] if you were able to talk about the Buddha's expedient teachings for as many eons as there are grains of sand in a river, you'd still never complete your explanation or get anywhere. All these are just like not-yet-severed barbs and chains." For Mazu, and for Chan generally, entering into meditative absorption or stillness and demonstrating scholarly brilliance are equally classed as overdoing it.

The absence of unambiguous and crucial marks—be they objective or subjective—would have made the identification of authentic Chan practitioners difficult, if not impossible. Some would argue that it was precisely the ability of Chan adepts to blend into any situation whatsoever that allowed the tradition to survive the traumas of the mid-eighth and ninth centuries. At the very least, it is clear that there were no freestanding Chan monasteries in China until well into the Song dynasty and that Chan practice customarily and compatibly took place within the same walls as Tiantai, Huayan, and Pure Land forms of Buddhist observance. Undoubtedly, it was this simple fact that made possible—and perhaps even inevitable—the kinds of syncretistic movements that took place, for example, in tenth-century Wuyue and that sought to construct hybrid Chan traditions. At bottom, the distinctive spirit of Chan practice rests on nothing more substantial than the readiness to perform everyday activities with unparalleled, interactive genius. Practicing Chan is just demonstrating, moment by moment, a unique force, quality, and direction of relationship: the realization of liberating intimacy.

The traditional literature of Chan offers hundreds of narrative snapshots of such relational transformation. Unfortunately, as anyone knows who has tried reading through Chan discourse records and public case (Chinese: *gongan;* Japanese: *koan*) collections like the *Gateless Frontier Pass* and the *Blue Cliff Record,* it is possible to stare for hours at such snapshots with a complete lack of comprehension. We may chuckle politely, like people who've heard an inside joke without the benefit of any insider knowledge. But we don't—and perhaps can't—really "get it."

Many commentators have taken to seeing the confounding effect of Chan *gongan* and encounter dialogues *(wenda)* as a central purpose of the stories themselves, pointing out that the intellect cannot access the full meaning of Chan liberation. And, indeed, realizing that rationality has proper limits is a kind of liberation. But the outbursts of mature Chan spirituality recorded in the *gongan* literature and discourse records cannot be reduced to this. That would be like looking at a family photo album of portraits and action shots, placed in no chronological order, and thinking that the point of the album is to drive home the incomprehensibility of familial ties. Family bonds may be inherently hard to understand, but the album is much more than an illustration of this fact. If one knows that some of the photos in the album are of weddings, while others are of birthday parties, graduations, athletic contests, school dances, or holiday dinners, one can begin to get a sense of how they fit together. The order that then emerges opens a growing sense of the meaning of family as practiced by these particular people over the course of several generations. Similarly, with a suitable organizing framework, one can bring the practice of Chan spirituality into personally meaningful focus.

For heuristic purposes, then, it is possible to identify three interlocking dimensions implied in the practice of Chan. First and foremost is an embodied understanding that (as Linji puts it) carrying out bodhisattva action often entails "facing the world and going crosswise." The specifics of our liberating activity cannot be predicated only on what has worked in the past. Innovation is essential. This is the ultimate stress of Huineng's teaching of the "readiness to awaken": Chan conduct—the practice of liberating relationships—involves realizing improvisational virtuosity or unprecedented skill in means. As I will show, this does not happen by itself, by chance, or by cultivating "good traits," but only through systematically relinquishing the roots of duality.

Second, it is clear that such virtuosity—a life and circumstances completely free of both obstructions and habits—requires a great deal of energy. Although breaking down obstructions and habits releases a great deal of energy, it often requires the skilled focusing and application of energy in the first place. A dam blocking the free flow of water might well erode on its own over time if it is not actively maintained. But if the water is needed now to irrigate parched fields, the dam must be broken through. The same is true for relational blockages. Moreover, to be always in a position to contribute to or enrich our situation as needed, we must be able to draw on practically unlimited wealth.

Although it is seldom directly addressed in the literature of Chan, relational virtuosity rests on a foundation of energy work without which even the best of intentions will fall short of their mark.

Finally, because such lively and open virtuosity is by nature responsive to situational particulars, it cannot be generically fostered or abstractly depicted. There is little or no use in talking about enlightenment. We can only be introduced to the taste of Chan spirituality through being present in situational demonstrations of the meaning of liberating relationships. It is for this reason that all Chan masters have stressed the need to find and enter the company of a good teacher. Only in this direct encounter are we able to recover for ourselves the full meaning of unobstructed appreciative and contributory virtuosity.

The remainder of this chapter will be devoted to seeing more precisely how relinquishing the roots of duality, energy work, and fulfilling the master-disciple relationship exemplify the practice of Chan spirituality. Although the discussion will be rooted in the historical emergence of Chan in China, I hope that it will indirectly serve as an analogue for how the spirit of Chan might also be translated into the idiom of our own life stories.

Relinquishing All Limits to Relevance, Responsibility, and Readiness: Chan Nonduality

In an irreducibly dynamic cosmos, appreciative and contributory virtuosity must be improvisational in nature. Improvisation is not, however, just a matter of acting without precedents. If that were so, then the random outbursts of a lunatic would qualify as improvisational genius, as would the first fumbling attempts of infants or children to engage and transform their situation. Improvisational virtuosity differs from these because it results in unprecedented and yet skillfully responsive conduct.

Chan and Zen masters have often stressed the importance of realizing "beginner's mind." In doing so, they are not urging blissful ignorance of the complexity of life or an infantile regression. Instead, they are encouraging us to realize freedom from the blockages of what is "known" and "certain." These mark the reality limit of our prior inquiries and present skills. And unless we go beyond it, we cannot conduct ourselves with improvisational virtuosity.

The beginner's mind of Chan can be compared to the thoughtless brilliance of a great athlete or master crafts worker. Like Chan bodhisattvas, they, too, often seem able—at least on the playing field or in the workshop—to do the impossible. But the brilliance of Chan mastery must illuminate any and all situations. Because of this, there can be no training in Chan that parallels the play-by-play drills of team athletes or the production work of the apprentice crafts worker. Chan virtuosity takes place on the infinite dramatic field of daily life—a field that has no sidelines or end zones where the action stops and where plans can be hatched and energy safely regained. We cannot train for Chan mastery, because there is not even a single moment between birth and death during which we are not playing for keeps.

Like the monk throttled by Linji and challenged to "speak!" our typical reaction to this quandary is withdrawal. We want to retreat a step or two back to consider options, gather information, and study the overall context of our situation. But time will not stop. The situation we set out to investigate and comprehend has ceased to exist even before we have completed this initiating thought. Unless we are willing to accept the consequences of acting on the basis of a present we imagine wholly in terms of a past we did not know well enough to respond to directly in the first place, we must skillfully respond, without hesitating, right now. For this, we must let go of any tightness, rigidity, or narrowness of attention. What is needed is a mind that is as clear and boundless as space. The Chan practice of realizing appreciative and contributory virtuosity can be seen, then, as the activation of nonduality: a systematic relinquishing of the horizons binding three qualitative fields: the field of what we consider relevant, the field of what we consider our responsibility, and the field of our own readiness.

The great Indian Buddhist philosopher Nagarjuna said that all things are relevant for those who realize emptiness. Chinese Buddhists combined this concept with the general Mahayana association of emptiness and interdependence: the emptiness of all things consists of their meaningful interdependence. Realizing the emptiness of things is thus realizing how each thing contributes to the meaning of all other things and how all things contribute, in turn, to each thing's own meaning. Fazang, China's most astute commentator on the *Huayan Sutra*, or *Flower Ornament Sutra*, explained its central teaching of emptiness by the mutual causation of ridge beams and rafters. The function or meaning of a ridge beam is to establish the high point of a roof and hold it aloft. But there can be no ridge beam in the absence of rafters that connect it to the walls of a building. At the same time, the function of rafters is to support the ridge beam and establish a base for the purlins onto which roofing tiles are attached. Before being assembled, there are pieces of wood, but no "rafters" or "ridge beams." Of course, the field of interdependence or mutual causation is not restricted to just the rafters and ridge beam. For example, there are neither rafters nor ridge beams without carpenters who cut them but also no carpenters unless wood is being cut into such functional shapes. Ultimately, each thing depends on all others for the meaning of being present as it is.

Relinquishing our horizons for relevance concretely expresses the emptiness of things. It is a process of erasing the boundaries imposed on the meaning of things by our customary relationships with them. Effectively, this process frees things to mean more than they otherwise could. But freeing things from the restrictions normally placed on what they can mean or contribute to our shared situation is to deepen our partnership and intimacy with them. It is realizing our own emptiness. By relinquishing our horizons for what we deem relevant in any given situation, we undermine our point of view, actively undercutting the conceit of independent existence and of being an actor or agent whose identity comes from exerting some measure of control over acted upon things and situations.

In doing so, we realize that our solutions to problems can only be as complete as our embrace of the relevance of all things. To some extent, this implies being attentive to the future or, more properly, the direction of things. Dumping waste into a lake or river is a solution only as long as the fish living in it are not relevant to our diet, as long as fresh water for irrigation and drinking is not needed, and as long as we don't care about what happens to whom downstream. Relinquishing our horizons for relevance attunes us to the needs of others and of our situation as a whole. At once, it widens the circle of our concern and deepens our ability to appreciate fully the resources our situation offers and the liberating potential of its opportunities and dangers.

All of this pivots on giving up the fixed distinctions that drive both our tendency toward neglect and our particular patterns of obsessive and habitual thinking. The process of relinquishing our horizons for relevance is thus what Chan Buddhists referred to as nonthinking. Its effect is realizing no-mind: the absence of any fixed dispositional perspectives and thus of anything to think about. The point is not to forgo all planning—if by that is meant simply envisioning ways to make sure that the relevant parts of our situation come together at the right time and the right place. It is not to become insentient like a stone or a dead tree. Huineng makes it clear that "if you do not think of the myriad things but always cause your thoughts to be cut off, you will be bound [and not liberated] by the Dharma." Practicing emptiness by relinquishing one's horizons for relevance means compassionately refusing to silence other things, refusing to pick and choose experiences according to self-centered likes and dislikes, and being able and willing to let go of what should work to realize artlessly what does work. It is actively reducing and resolving suffering by removing the blockages that keep all things from taking care of themselves and expressing their buddha-nature: an orientation toward liberating relationships.

There is a danger in this opportunity for freeing all things. Knowing that all things are empty or free of any fixed or essential nature can wrongly, but easily, be used to justify doing nothing on their behalf—an excuse for refraining from acting compassionately for the benefit of others. Appealing to the relevance of all things can slip into a belief in the relativity of all things and a conviction that even suffering is not inherently suffering. Ignorance may be seen as not necessarily bad. Crime may be seen as not intrinsically wrong. Social ills, war, and structural violence may be seen as simply thus and in no need of correcting.

This kind of perverse interpretation of nonduality was very early denounced by Mahayana Buddhists. To counter it, the teaching of karma was used to stress our dramatic interdependence with all things and the central role of our values and intentions in the shape of our world. Our situation may not be fixed or essential in nature but, as an irreducibly karmic situation, it is always one for which we have responsibility. This understanding of karma led some Mahayana Buddhists to claim that our situation is, at bottom, mind-only. Since there are no independently existing things, and since all things are meaningfully interdependent, our world must always be consonant with the tone of our own minds.

Seeing that this is so is to practice relinquishing our horizons for responsibility. Thus, while some Chan masters stressed the teaching of no-mind with their students, others—most explicitly and notably, Huangbo—stressed the teaching of one-mind. Their point was to affirm the absence of any ultimate boundaries separating me and you or our situation and theirs, and to insist on the moral implications of this aspect of nonduality for Buddhist practice. Thus, Huangbo constantly refers to enlightenment or awakening as "a silent bond" through which—no matter what is happening—all things are revealed as "entirely oneself" or "one's own family" and so as one's own doing or karma. Chan awakening, said Mazu, is like becoming the ocean into which all streams and rivers flow. The awakened do not disown any aspect of their situation. They do not blame others for their ills or reject some aspect of the present situation as the responsibility or doing of someone else. Rather, they draw all things near and transform their meaning. Doing this is the bodhisattva practice of embracing all things in the ongoing work of purification and clearing that is buddha-nature.

In this spirit of overcoming all horizons for responsibility, Huineng thus insisted that a true Chan practitioner truly does not see any errors in the world. "If you see wrongs in the world, it is your own wrongdoing that is affirmed. We are to blame for the wrongs of others just as we are to blame for our own." In the context of the Buddhist teaching of emptiness, this practice brings about a realization of the irreducibly shared nature of our situation and its meaning. This radical affirmation of oneness with all beings is an ongoing exercise in moral nonduality. Its success pivots on having sufficient virtue to be able to contribute responsibly to directing each and every situation from samsara to nirvana, from isolation and suffering to liberating intimacy—an ability that can only be exercised with others.

There is, however, a liability in formulating the teaching that all is one-mind or "mind-only." Granted that we live in a beginningless cosmos, affirming the nondual presence of all things and the inescapable role of our own values and intentions—our own karma—in shaping the present situation, we may be tempted to think that there is little hope of realizing the bodhisattva ideal. If the karmic seeds for today's myriad ills and troubles were planted over an infinite amount of time and are only now bearing fruit, how could we ever hope to make progress in uprooting the basis of all suffering? Can we really hope to purify and clear the world and thus our own minds in less time than it took to "dirty" them? After all, our own minds are being dirtied practically every instant of the day by the dust of the world. How could we ever hope—as things are at present—to live the bodhisattva life?

Chan's answer is, simply by doing so. The teaching of *dunwu* affirms our capacity to relinquish our horizons of readiness in active demonstration of our buddha-nature. It is an explicit rejection of setting up awakening as a goal to be reached when our mind's storehouse has been cleared of all its ill karmic seeds and we are clear and supple enough to engage freely each and every situation as bodhisattvas. When Shenxiu suggests that Chan practice is an ongoing process of clearing and purifying the mind of polluting dusts that alight in the course of day-to-day experience, Huineng wants to know who makes "polluting dusts" in the first place. If all things have no essential or fixed nature, what makes this experience polluting and that one sublime? What makes one thing secular and another one sacred? Isn't this our own doing, right here and now—something we can stop if only we are ready to do so?

But the Chan denial of objective barriers to liberation is not simply a rehearsal of the teaching of emptiness. It is the affirmation that awakening is not something that can be blocked by so many moments of time or by how we habitually think, feel, speak, and act. Awakening can only be ignored or resisted. The key to liberating all beings successfully is not infinitely extensive and unrelenting training or effort but simply horizonless readiness *(dun)*.

In keeping with this understanding of practice, Chan master Huihai stated that "*dun* is the readiness to do away with misleading thoughts"—thoughts that lead us to neglect what is present right here with us—while "*wu* is awakening to the absence of anything to be attained." The method for accomplishing *dunwu* is "responding to sit-

uations with no-mind" and hence without any limiting horizons. Huihai refers to this response as "the perfection of offering."

As mentioned above, the Chinese word for "relinquishing" suggests not only parting with something but also bestowing and giving
alms or sacred offerings. In the practice of Chan, we do not give up the
tools of our trade, our food, or our relationships with others. Instead,
we yield and offer the energy that has until now been bound up in our
habitual maintenance of self, others, likes, and dislikes. The release of
this energy signals our manifest readiness to realize that this very place
were we stand, sit, walk, or lie down is the *bodhimandala,* or place of
awakening. Right here and now is the Pure Land.

Our normal tendency, even if we assume responsibility for our
situation, is to defer or put off acting until we are ready. We believe
that we are not yet strong enough or knowledgeable enough or fully
enough aware and present. We feel we that must train for a while still
or at least wait until the time is right or until circumstances cooperate.
It is with this kind of rationalization in mind that Chan masters constantly denied that Chan depended on cultivation or any kind of repet-
itive training. Chan is directly manifesting, in our conduct, the confidence or faith that all things share the same enlightening nature. There
is no need to set up goals for future attainment but only to give up the
root duality of who is or is not ready for awakening.

The opportunity for doing so is right before us every moment. This
is true because the Pure Land is not a place existing somewhere else
but, according to Chan, a quality of commitment and attention. In traditional Mahayana circles, the Pure Land is portrayed as a birth situation lying between our current life circumstances and full enlightenment. It is a transitional space through which passage is possible in one
direction only—to complete and unsurpassed awakening. Granted
that all things are empty, however, it is clear that no situation can be
inherently other than the Pure Land. If our situation appears as something other than the Pure Land, it is only because we do not see it as
open to the meaning of liberation. The Pure Land is, in other words,
not a fixed destination to be sought, but a particular direction for the
meaning of our situation as a whole, right now. All that is lacking is
our own readiness *(dun)* for realizing this. Huineng thus insists that it
is our own minds—in the process of purifying our situation—that

constitute the Pure Land. The meaning of our situation ultimately pivots on nothing else.

The path to any specific destiny or goal can be blocked. But nothing can stop us from facing in the proper direction, from reorienting the dramatic navigation of our situation. Demonstrating unwavering commitment and ceaselessly exercising attentive virtuosity are all that is required. They form the root offering or contribution we can make to the welfare of all beings. By continuously relinquishing, as they arise, all horizons for relevance, responsibility, and readiness, we live the lives of bodhisattvas demonstrating unlimited skill in the means of realizing truly liberating relationships. Only by doing so are we in no position to experience the resistance of things—and ourselves—to awakening. Giving rise to no fixed point of view and no horizons, we find ourselves moving naturally in the direction of expressing appreciative and contributory virtuosity. That, after all, is our buddhanature.

Meditation as Energy Work

It is often stated that the psychological depth of Buddhism was very appealing to the Chinese. Buddhism offered a sophisticated treatment of a dimension of human experience that China's indigenous thought systems had left largely unaddressed. But, in fact, this factor seems to have played a relatively minor role in China's adoption of Buddhism. Of the major schools of Chinese Buddhism, none was centered on the psychologically rich commentarial literature from India. Instead, they coalesced around texts—the *Lotus, Flower Ornament, Pure Land,* and *Vimalakirti* sutras, for example—that practically ignored subjective experience in favor of extensive examples of skilled conduct. And although Chinese Buddhists did write about attention training and meditation, their approach reflected a similar bias. Comparatively little time was devoted to examining the extensive and complex Indian systems for ranking levels and degrees of contemplative and concentrative experience.

Chan was no exception to this tendency to discount experiential results in favor of the socially demonstrated effects of Buddhist practice. A standard Chan definition of meditation was "meeting situations without obstruction." Although a psychological reading of this notion could be forced, for Chinese practitioners of Chan the point was clear: meditation is the body of wisdom, the function of which is skilled and beneficial interaction.

This understanding of meditation is thoroughly Chinese. It reflects Daoist sensibilities going back to the centuries before the introduction of Buddhism to China that treat all things as focuses of qualitative energies. As mentioned earlier, unlike Western scientific and philosophical traditions, the Chinese tradition settled very early on a cosmology in which all things consist of blends of energy *(qi)* that is primarily and most relevantly qualitative. The basic qualities of *yin* and *yang* were themselves viewed as correlative in nature, not absolute opposites, and were each held to be present in some degree in all things and situations. For early Daoists, cosmic harmony was nothing other than the free circulation of these qualities of *qi.* As stated by Zhuangzi, "When *qi* circulates freely, the myriad things take care of themselves."

This understanding of cosmic harmony was applied as well to the harmony of the human body and to social health. Traditional Chinese medicine and sociopolitical theory rested on a shared model: ills result from interruptions or imbalances of *qi* and are healed or treated through restoring its natural pattern of circulation. Early Chinese meditative traditions explicitly concerned themselves with unblocking and balancing *qi* for the combined purpose of bringing about personal health and correct relationships. Meditative adepts were not, in general, renowned for having mystical experiences or intensely altered states of consciousness. Rather, their primary mark of distinction was entirely public: an ability to induce harmony in others without saying a word. "Just standing alongside others," Zhuangzi claimed, "they can induce people to change until correct relationships . . . have found their way into every home."

In terms that would later resonate deeply with Buddhist teachings, Zhuangzi identified the key to this ability as not making the judgment "it is this or it is not." Meditative adepts or sages bring to an end the continual wounding that comes with the imposition of fixed distinctions. Their central practice was referred to as "fasting the heart-mind" —refraining from indulging our usual diet of likes and dislikes. As one syncretistic Han dynasty text, the *Huainanzi,* puts it, when meditation deepens, not only will the myriad affairs take care of themselves, one "knows without studying, sees without looking, and accomplishes everything without doing anything."

In summary, pre-Buddhist Chinese traditions understood meditation as energy work aimed at dissolving the habitual self and opening ourselves to conduct that is spontaneous and nurturing—conduct that restores the natural capacity of all things to contribute to their shared harmony and welfare. The point is not an exalting experience of some sort—even though such experiences may, at times, occur—but realizing the kind of thoughtless virtuosity and charisma that characterizes a leader who artlessly draws out the best of any situation. Meditation clarifies and enhances the quality of interdependence.

From its earliest years, Chan was renowned as the Chinese Buddhist school or lineage most strongly committed to the centrality of meditation. In fact, the written character "*chan*" was used as a rough transliteration for the Indian Sanskrit term for meditative absorption, "*dhyana.*" But, if Chan can truly be referred to as a meditation school, it is in a decidedly Chinese sense of meditation. Making use of extensive common ground with early Daoist thought and practice, Chan Buddhist teachers explicitly and almost exclusively focused on the transformative effect of meditation on our situation as a whole. Like their largely Daoist predecessors, they remained almost completely silent about its subjective or experiential dimension. The function of meditation was to do the bodhisattva work of changing the quality of interdependence obtaining at any given moment, shifting it in the direction of truly liberating intimacy.

Effecting this transformation means being always able to complement the prevailing pattern of *qi* that characterizes our situation. In some dramatic contexts, this will involve an almost delicate offering of *yin*. Other contexts will require a thunderous contribution of *yang.* Not only must bodhisattvas sense—like freely improvising virtuoso musicians—precisely what will work, they must be in the immediate position to channel or release just that quality and amount of *qi* needed to transform a uniquely troubled situation into a liberating one.

Because the Chinese associated emotions and temperament with different qualities and configurations of *qi,* the virtuosity required of bodhisattvas is not intellectually abstract or purely physical, but dramatic. Huineng thus insists that awakening not take place apart from the passions but directly in and among them. In the tragic circumstances that prevailed when Chan shock tactics were being most forcefully developed, it would have required great courage and confidence to remain fully and emotionally engaged with unfailing readiness to awaken. The energy resources needed deftly to change the meaning of such circumstances would have been titanic. Indeed, only "true persons with no rank" would be able to demonstrate such appreciative and contributory virtuosity, transforming everywhere they go into the place of awakening.

The contrary of this fluid and infinitely enriching presence is familiar to all of us: being blocked, hesitant, wary, or unsure in a continuously failing effort to make sense out of things and control what is happening. It is feeling that we lack some insight or energy needed to transform our situation properly, believing that more time must pass or more practice or planning undertaken before we can really respond as needed. Avoiding such a way of being present cannot be a matter of exercising self control. The desire for control already announces that we have forfeited true intimacy with our situation to stand over, against, or apart from it in some essential way. Ironically, the distance needed to leverage one's situation into the shape one independently wants is precisely what makes it appear in need of control. It is the distance that appears when we don't know what to do or whether the control we are exerting is properly directed. This mind of doubt is a dramatic vacuum into which energy is drawn from everything nearby. In effect, it impoverishes our situation and renders it incapable of taking care of itself.

According to Chan, we must instead put a stop to all manner of picking and choosing. Thus, many Chan masters referred to the function of meditation as realizing the "great, round mirror wisdom." This is not an appeal for cultivating a capacity to reflect accurately on or display knowledge about the world. In Chan rhetoric, the distinctive nature of mirrors is that they neither reject nor hold onto anything. In mirrors, all things can be freely present, coming and going without obstruction, leaving no traces. The mirror metaphor thus links wisdom with a capacity for fully receiving and openly offering back everything that comes to us. As the "body" of wisdom, Chan meditation is not about properly reflecting or representing how things are. It is about shining with the contributory light of all things, immediately focusing and blending their diverse energies and returning them into meaningful and harmonious circulation.

Understanding meditation in terms of energy work, Chan teachers often associated the metaphor of the "great, round mirror wisdom" with the ocean seal *samadhi*. Although this mixing of metaphors— the mirror and the ocean—might be considered odd, it makes perfect sense in the context of a *qi* cosmology. Before entering China's scientific and philosophical canon, the word "*qi*" originally referred to the quality of movements and moods associated with waters, vapors, and clouds. The languid gurgling of fog-shrouded mountain springs marked a certain quality of *qi*. So did the roaring of cataract-producing waterfalls, the rumbling boulder crashes of a summer thunderstorm, the silent swirl of a snow flurry, the howling of a hurricane gale, and the splashing heartbeat rhythms of breaking waves. As the center of the circulatory system joining heaven and earth, the ocean receives all waters, eventually giving birth to clouds that carry purified vapor to every part of the globe, where eventually it condenses and falls, shaping the land and nurturing all living things. As the ocean was understood as cleansing and purifying the muddy river waters flowing into it, the *samadhi,* or attentive virtuosity, of the Chan meditative adept was understood as being continuously open to all things and capable of restoring their original nature.

Clearly, if we are busy expending all of our energy in search of this or that culminating experience, we will not be in a position to accord with our situation and respond as needed. It is the nature of seeking certain things that it requires excluding from awareness a great many others. The single method consistently offered for the practice of Chan meditation is not seeking anything and welcoming whatever comes your way. As Huangbo put it, this is the only sure way of "conserving the mind's energy"—the only way of insuring that the energy needed for appreciative and contributory brilliance is continuously available. When we insist on trying to control our present or on imagining better things from the past or in the future, we effectively drain the present situation of value and place ourselves in poverty. When we give up all seeking, we stop draining our situation. Nor are we drained by it. Because the flow of energy into and through us never ceases, we are always in a position of benefiting and being benefited by others. Through making the karma of appreciation, we find ourselves profoundly and immeasurably enriched. This is the realization behind Mahayana Buddhist representations of bodhisattvas as adorned with jewels and fine clothes in a live paradise of gem-bearing trees and ambrosial streams.

Huangbo tells his students that if they had at all times just learned and practiced no-mind, they would have fully arrived some time ago. They would have realized what is meant when the Buddha is referred to as the "thus come one," or Tathagata. But "because your energy is so low, you're not capable of the readiness to leap over [to awakening]. If you manage to put in three or five or perhaps ten years, however, you'll certainly attain an entry and be able to go on spontaneously." That is, it will be possible to respond as needed without making any special effort. It's only due to a chronic lack of appropriate *qi,* or energy, that this is not possible. It's like taking perfect aim and shooting an arrow only to watch it fall to earth, far short of the target, because the energy we applied to it with our muscles and bow is prematurely expended.

One might imagine Huangbo's students asking what exactly they should be doing for the next three to five years. How can we tap into the energy reserves needed to demonstrate horizonless readiness for awakening? In all likelihood, they would have been answered with a blow from Huangbo's stick, a kick in the shins, or a dismissive wisecrack about them wanting to "add legs to a snake." His point would have been, your question already has picking and choosing built into it. What question could there be about what to do unless you are in two minds about what is best? Realizing that, you should stop asking questions and get to work. Readiness is not something to put off for tomorrow or the next day. There is no such thing as getting ready and no time for imagining further obstructions.

Chan masters often cried out to their students that they were living in a burning house. The image is drawn from a story in the *Lotus Sutra.* By offering to give his children toy wagons and pet animals, a father is able to ply his children quickly out of the family home—which, unknown to them as they play indoors, is going up in flames all around them. He does not try to convince them of the truth that the fire will soon consume them but concentrates instead on what will deliver them to safety. In dealing with students at play seeking enlightenment, Chan masters came to employ rather more imperative "skillful means" to draw the "tiger out of its lair." Mazu's punches, Huangbo's slaps, and Linji's shouts are all examples of such shocking means of bringing students fully enough into the present to demonstrate their own readiness to awaken.

Such challenging responses, however, were by no means the only ones available in Chan circles. The most commonly prescribed method for restoring the free circulation of *qi* was "stilling the mind" or realizing a "nonmoving mind." A mind that is worried and rushing here and there in search of a "solution" to the problem of doubt or the problem of inadequate energy is effectively closed to the present moment and in no position to receive anything. To suggest a metaphor, it is like digging frantically for water in a mountain hollow on a gently rainy day. Water is welling up slowly from a deep underground spring, but we are scraping up and tossing dirt out so fast it never has a chance to collect as a clean, drinkable supply. Rainwater showers the area and is trickling down into the hollow, but we are so busy digging, we are completely unaware of it. Again, it cannot collect because we keep throwing it up out of the hollow in our desperate search for water. A more common metaphor in Mahayana Buddhist literature is that of someone rushing all over in search of a "lost" wish-fulfilling gem that is actually stuck to his own forehead.

It is no simple matter, however, to still the mind to the point of not seeking anything and to sustain this process continuously. Like other Chinese Buddhists, Chan practitioners also had recourse to a wide array of intermediary attention-training techniques for stilling the mind. Among these were simple mindfulness practices like following the breath that are still undertaken in Chan, Son, and Zen training today. Other widespread techniques were chanting sutras, visualizing Buddhist images or symbols, ritual prostrations and offerings of incense and food, and reciting either the Buddha's name or the name of a renowned bodhisattva like Guanyin.

Carried out over time with sufficiently great intensity, such techniques can forcefully break through our habits of thought and perception. As attention energy is continuously directed to the breath, a mantra, chanting, or a visualized image, energy is directed away from its customary paths in our body-mind system. By sustaining this attentive focus—for hours, days, or weeks at a time—we "fast" the heart-mind. Like a garden that receives no water, our pattern of habits undergoes great stress and—as a system—can eventually disintegrate. The result is a release of energy that was previously bound up in making and maintaining the kinds of distinctions needed to support both our various senses of self—our purportedly independent identities—and the props they require.

During meditation retreats, it is not uncommon for such breakthroughs to occur. For some people, the result will be a cathartic experience that dissolves a long-standing emotional or conceptual blockage. For others, after several days of sitting, it may be that the pain in their knees and back suddenly is perceived as no pain at all. The same sensations are still present, but not the experience referred to as "pain." For still others, there may be a burst of "mystical" insight—a feeling of sudden oneness with all things, perhaps, or the falling away of all burdens.

Similar turnabouts can take place in daily life and not just in the meditation hall. In all cases, the Chan reading of such releases and reversals is not that they are ends in themselves. Rather, they are seen in functional terms as opening new dimensions for freely attending to and caring for our situation. Chan masters like Linji thus strenuously rejected the idea that Chan meditation has anything finally to do with sitting in quiet places and withdrawing from the affairs of the world. If chasing around in search of enlightenment or liberation is counterproductive, so is seeking out peace and quiet or cathartic experiences. Meditation is for the purpose of being able to "enter fire without being burnt, going into water without drowning, and frolicking in the three deepest hells as if at a fairground." The point is not to live the life of a recluse, but "joining things" in a life of unhindered, compassionate engagement.

Indeed, there is a great danger if the energies released through attention training do not freely circulate. Chan teachers regularly warn their students about the possibility of "meditation sickness." By diligently carrying out attention training, it is not only that habitual systems of thought, feeling, and action are starved of the energy needed to operate as usual. These systems are integral to the way of life we have come to know as normal, no matter how dissatisfactory it sometimes seems to us. Indeed, the resistance that arises from the world when we meet it with habitual attention is crucial to the formation of our egos and overall sense of self. The breakdown of particularly mental and emotional habits can effectively leave us feeling profoundly uprooted even in situations that previously seemed comfortable and secure.

Moreover, qualities of energy that were previously blocked out become manifestly present. With this, our sensory relationships are greatly extended. In some cases, this might itself lead to sudden changes in our "luck" or to a noticeably altered capacity for normal daily functioning. In others, it might play a role in inducing us to place ourselves in situations where we end up dramatically in over our heads, our compassion proving greater than our actual skill in means. In much less common cases, it might lead to the development of so-called paranormal abilities like clairaudience, clairvoyance, and the perception of people's past karma. In all such cases, if one's practice is profoundly compassionate and selfless, these energies and abilities eventually open new opportunities for liberating revisions of our situation. But if we have remained effectively self-centered through the course of our training, the energies flowing into us along these "new" channels can actually be difficult or impossible to release properly into general circulation. If directed arrogantly or selfishly, the karma created can be very dangerous to all involved. Meditation, carried out in the absence of guidance toward wisdom and moral clarity is, by itself, no guarantee of Buddhist awakening or liberation.

Mazu's student Huihai goes so far as to warn that if someone claims to possess "proofs of achievement" and meditative "attainments," we should see this as evidence of them being arrogant and attached to misleading views. Such persons do not purify and clear those who come into contact with them, restoring their original nature and the free circulation of the Dao. On the contrary, they effectively obstruct the Dao. The root condition of Chan realization is having no self to which "proofs" and "attainments" could be affixed. In the absence of this mirrorlike humility, our "attainments" will come only at the cost of draining our situation of the energy and resources needed for it to take care of itself. We may succeed in controlling our situation through the acquisition of new perceptual abilities and energy resources. But in doing so, we make karma for being in situations that are increasingly in need of control. Unchecked, we can create the karmic equivalent of a black hole that swallows everything that comes near and that neither illuminates nor gives anything in return.

Thus, Huangbo insists that "having no mind is nondraining wisdom"—the demonstrated capacity for always being in a position to respond as needed, in ways that neither deplete our own resources or those of our situation. The relational quality of this "perfection of offering" is clearly articulated in Mazu's simple statement that "a buddha is capable of *ren* (beneficent authority). Having skills and wisdom regarding the excellent nature of dangers and opportunities, buddhas are able to break through the net of doubts snaring all sentient beings . . . without obstruction in whatever they do."

When meditation training is undertaken with the skilled guidance of a master who is able to foster the realization of no-self, it brings about a capacity for responding as needed in ways that do not meet resistance and do not require us to exercise any special control. As indicated by Mazu's use of the Confucian term "*ren*," a key to realizing our buddha-nature through Chan practice involves being profoundly present with and for others. In the context of Chan practice, this concerned presence is formalized in daily offerings of water, rice, and incense; in biweekly ceremonies tied to the lunar cycle and including recollections of one's ancestors; in special ceremonies and practices associated with the Buddha's birth, enlightenment, and *parinirvana*, or passing away; and in other day-to-day ritual observances.

These and other informal acts of kindness and offering serve to build Chan practitioners' base of virtue. Through them, we learn to exercise our buddha-nature directly and to help it fully mature. By regularly making the karma of contribution, the self empties itself. The energies that have been sustaining its existence or standing apart from all things are released. And through this process, our situation becomes a horizonless field of virtue, at once empowered and empowering.

In an inherently dynamic and karmic cosmos, however, true virtue implies virtuosity. While ritually building a basis of virtue is profoundly empowering, bodhisattva action often entails immediate, unprecedented, and yet liberating responsiveness. Such action means, first, that virtue must be built and exercised at all times and in all places. Otherwise, our responsive resources will be practically limited and, eventually, insufficient. But in addition to having sufficient reserves of virtue, we also must have a keen sense—even if only implicit—of how to revise the karma present in any given situation. Ultimately, the pattern of energy flows and blockages characterizing any situation are consonant with patterns of value and intention maintained by all those involved in it. Horizonless readiness for awakening thus involves what might be called dramatic virtuosity or unlimited skill in karmic improvisation.

Here, we find a key difference between the Buddhist practice of offering and ritual sacrifice. Ritual sacrifice presupposes an order in the cosmos that is at least relatively fixed and typically requires a strict adherence to traditional precedent. Although rituals must to some extent be personalized, they cannot be made up on the spot. Their efficacy is not based on luck or momentary genius but on the historical discovery of constant principles of interaction between the forces that manage cosmic order and the human community. In any particular case, it is not necessary to take situational uniqueness into ritual account to achieve desirable results. On the contrary, all that is needed is to identify correctly and execute the type of sacrificial ritual that is appropriate.

To conduct ourselves fully as bodhisattvas, however, typical responses are seldom good enough. Although regular occasions for ritually choreographed practices of offering are very much a part of both monastic and lay Buddhist observance, these do not express either the full range or the culmination of Buddhist offering. Instead, they serve as a matrix for cultivating important qualities of both sentiment and attention. These qualities then must be uniquely deployed in any particular situation in ways sensitive to the currents of meaning already present in it and in ways consonant with the bodhisattva vow of turning all situations from samsara to nirvana. At the very least, this requires being open to the full range of dramatic or karmic currents presently contributing to how things are going, and being creative and flexible enough to harmonize them skillfully. The conduct of a bodhisattva must be, in other words, thoroughly ethical in the sense of being utterly sensitive to the values and customary dispositions that are characteristic of any given situation as it has come to be. Because no culture or situation is fixed and unchanging, however, in its fullest sense and expression, Buddhist offering must be improvised here and now in the midst of daily life.

For this, there can be no prescriptions. It cannot be taught. No written text can show how it is done. Even if we are present in situations where dramatic virtuosity is being exercised, it is almost impossible to see what is taking place. Often, it is only after the karmic resolution has been realized that we can identify what had, all along, been skillfully leading up to it. But because every situation is unique, even this kind of understanding cannot be generalized effectively. To realize truly what Huineng meant by saying that "it is precisely Buddhist practice that is Buddha"—that is, to realize the meaning of Chan—continuously relinquishing of our horizons of relevance, responsibility, and readiness is fundamental. To be able to do so, specific skills in offering—gained through both meditative training and other forms of energy work—are necessary. Together these establish a base for realizing that Chan means unfaltering, virtuosic response to need in a continuous direction. But they are not sufficient. Realizing full sympathetic resonance *(ganying)* with all things cannot be done in isolation or alone. Finally, the meaning of Chan spirituality and practice cannot be disclosed in the abstract or at second hand. It can become clear only by immediately participating in the utter moral clarity of realizing truly liberating relationships.

Moral Clarity and Chan Awakening

For the Chan tradition, the teaching encounter became the paradigmatic site for the realization of liberating relationships. As demonstrated in the encounter dialogues and public cases that form the core literature of Chan awakening, liberation does not imply any sort of metaphysical border crossing—an absolute and final achievement of freedom from all things. Rather, it means freely relating with all things in redirecting the present situation, as it has come to be, toward the meaningful resolution of all suffering or trouble. Chan awakening is demonstrating profoundly situated virtuosity.

Because of this, there are no clear and lasting principles of action to be gleaned from reading the literary distillations of Chan awakening, no prescriptions for how to turn a situation from samsara toward nirvana. As each situation is, at some level, dramatically unique, the same must hold for its enlightening, interpersonal revision. There is a striking lack of unanimity among Chan teachings. They are not, fundamentally, expressions of a singular and universally applicable truth but systematically responsive ways of *truing* a particular situation. As such, Chan teachings are not correct for all persons, at all times, and in all places. They are correctives appropriate for this person, at this time, in this place.

In reading the literature of Chan, this state of affairs can be quite confusing. Huineng exhorts his students to see their own true natures and realize their own minds as the Pure Land. Huangbo tells his students to realize no-mind, and Linji insists that his students drop both mind and no-mind to realize what it means to be a true person of no rank. On the one hand, this situation arises out of a realization of the need to match teachings with students. Audiences make a difference. On the other hand, it evidences sensitivity to the fact that all concepts are constructed or conventional and can, therefore, be deconstructed or used in unconventional ways. There can be no final formulation of the truth.

As the literature of Chan awakening developed in the late Tang and early Song dynasties, the impossibility of formulating any ultimate statement of truth became a guiding feature of commentaries on the encounter dialogues and public cases of past masters in the tradition. Since a once enlightening response cannot be so always and everywhere, not only is it possible to correct Chan masters of the past, doing so is practically an imperative. Thus, while Huineng is said to have corrected two monks arguing in a monastery courtyard about what is moving, the wind or the flag, informing them that it is mind that is moving, he is "hit" by later Chan masters who point out the implicit dualism of making a moving mind and nonmoving objects.

Although Chan masters are "homegrown buddhas" capable of offering whatever is needed to shift a given situation in the direction of liberating intimacy among all things, they are not able to save all beings at the same time or in the same way once and for all. In one sense, there should be nothing surprising about this. Even the historical Buddha did not claim literal omniscience and omnipotence. But it does require serious consideration of the meaning of the bodhisattva vow to save all sentient beings. If Chan masters have horizonless compassion and practically limited knowledge and abilities, will they not have to choose whom to work with and whom not? Will they not have to decide—given their own background and capabilities—whom they can save and whom they cannot? And if this is so, how can Chan insist that awakening is beyond all picking and choosing?

The most highly influential and respected Chan masters were typically those who developed the most distinctive—almost idiosyncratic—personal styles. Much as virtuoso musicians tend to specialize in a single instrument, playing it with a unique tone and sensibility, Chan masters typically specialized in characteristic forms of relational dynamics, making skilled use of a set of concepts and techniques with which they were exceptionally fluent.

Practically, this made it natural for them to develop teaching partnerships—like that between Huangbo and Dayu—sharing students for whom the differences between masters could make quite a fruitful difference. More important, however, the willingness to be uniquely oneself is also the most direct way of realizing one's emptiness or relevance for all things. "True persons of no rank" are not people who constantly change who they are. Rather, they are capable of fully being themselves, offering without hesitation or hindrance whatever they can in a way that works.

Being ourselves one hundred percent is emptying ourselves of all impediments to contributing to our situation as needed. It means expending no energy on checking ourselves, wasting no time picking the right method or choosing the right partners or deciding on the proper moment to act. Doing so, there can be no gaps in our engagement of our situation, no dramatic blind spots. Indeed, only in this way is it possible to present no resistance to the free circulation of energy through our situation and at the same time manifest uninterrupted dramatic clarity—an unwavering sense of liberating direction.

Here lies the great importance for Chan of the apocryphal treatise *Awakening of Mahayana Faith*. According to this text, the Mahayana path of the bodhisattva means having utter confidence in the suchness or buddha-nature of all things. Such confidence or faith effectively dissolves the need to be concerned with the particular facts of a situation, with what we have to offer, and with whether it is enough or not. Concerns of this sort only announce that we are not, at this moment, offering anything at all. Indulging in them will only further block the very situation we are attempting to open. Realizing complete faith or confidence in the one true nature of all things is realizing what it means to relate freely with all things without any hindrance or hesitation.

Granted that all things have the same true nature, all relationships are capable of turning in the direction of liberation. And given this, it is not what one offers that is most crucial but the quality and intention of one's offering. In a cosmos that is irreducibly dramatic and relational, saving all sentient beings is a direction—a distinctive meaning for a situation as a whole. The bodhisattva's vow is to infuse this meaning into all situations. In Chan, carrying out this vow means continuously relinquishing our horizons for relevance, responsibility, and readiness—realizing appreciative and contributory virtuosity.

The karma thus created is in many ways remarkable. The usual tendency is to try to make things better by managing one's situation, exerting some measure of control over how things turn out. But this kind of karma, in spite of good intentions we may have, commits us to a cycle where the better we get at controlling how things turn out, the more opportunity we will have to do so. This means living in situations that are always in need of further control. As our ability to control our situation increases, however, we find ourselves living in an increasingly controlled environment. Finally, we find ourselves living in the most controlled environment possible—in other words, a prison. By contrast, the better we get at contributing or offering to our situation, the more opportunity we will have for contributing. The more opportunity there is for contributing, however, the more we must be able to contribute. The karma created here is that, as our practice of offering or contribution deepens, we will find ourselves more and more valuably situated.

It is this sort of dynamic that underlies the story of the Chan master who did "not much of anything" and yet whose presence seemingly allowed all the diverse elements in his situation to harmonize freely.

By simply being thoroughly himself, he was already helping. Stopping to reflect on whether this is the best way of helping in all situations or a fully sufficient one is already to stop offering. Removing ourselves from our situation to stand apart in judgment of it, however momentarily, is to project before us an enclosing horizon of readiness. We are then in no position to demonstrate our readiness for awakening *(dunwu),* in no position to accord with our situation, responding as needed.

Whether living in the monastery or in lay society, Chan practitioners have always been enjoined by masters of the tradition to keep the bodhisattva precepts and to commit themselves to a meticulously ethical engagement with their situation. At the same time, they have been assured that the morality of Chan is not based on deciding what should be done but on offering so continuously and so well that there is no space and no need for making such decisions. It is a morality of lived nonduality that is not about realizing particular and prescribed states of affairs—now promoting the good and now dispelling the bad—but about immediately and directly benefiting what cannot be benefited and doing what cannot be done.

CHAPTER 7

Chan Now? Why and for Whom?

The story of Chan's early development is but one of many that could be drawn from the history of Buddhism. Chan's story is, perhaps, more colorful than most. Many of its main characters are so convincingly vibrant that it is easy to believe they are our own, often shocking, contemporaries. Although woven together in a culture and a historical setting remarkably different from our own, it is a story that rings with familiarity. Filled with utterly human passion and humor, it is welcoming in a way that is rare among traditional narratives of spiritual beginnings.

The story of Chan is, then, a good one. But, aside from that positive judgment about its own narrative of origin, why should we study Chan itself? What particular relevance does it have for us here and now in the first decade of the twenty-first century?

These are not easy questions to answer. As a scholar, I find the historical precedents for Chan fascinating. From this vantage, for example, Chan is a wonderfully rich case for studying what happens when value systems cross cultural boundaries. As such, it can shed useful light on such varied contemporary concerns as the exercise of religious tolerance, the accommodation of apparently contrary demands for secularity and sacredness, and what might happen as non-Western societies are infused with the values associated with democracy and civil society. It can provide equally useful perspectives from which to consider the role of vernacular narrative in the transmission of religious values, the process of challenging and consolidating authority, and such ethical issues as the moral imperative for improvisation.

But these reasons for studying Chan remain consciously—and perhaps conscientiously—on the sidelines of what Chan has always considered to be its own mission: to induce each and every one of us to demonstrate our own readiness for truly liberating intimacy. For a Buddhist practitioner, it is the sincerity and courage with which this mission is carried out that is most remarkable about Chan. The history of Chan is important but only because it affords such rich resources for articulating the indomitable spirit of Chan's mission. To a Buddhist practitioner it is clear that the contemporary relevance of Chan does not lie in what it tells us about our current situation, but in how it helps us to transform it. Practicing Chan means moment by moment opening and extending our own capacities for appreciative and contributory virtuosity, skillfully offering them for the benefit of all beings here in the midst of our own unique stories.

Doing so is at the same time to open and, eventually, to relinquish our own horizons for relevance, responsibility, and readiness. It is—for the purpose of discerning the root conditions of trouble or suffering—to question our own presuppositions vigilantly, undertaking a critical evaluation not only of our own values and intentions but of those prevailing in the situations in which we find ourselves. The improvisational genius that is so crucial to the practice and spirit of Chan is not a matter of doing what comes easily or acting on momentary whims. That is what we normally have in mind when we subscribe to an association of freedom with individual autonomy. We anticipate being able to do pretty much what we want, when and as we want. Viewed through the Buddhist lens of karma, this kind of control-biased freedom is a primary cause of suffering. It sentences us to that ever-deepening cycle: the better we get at getting what we want, the better we get at wanting; but the better we get at wanting, the better we get at getting what we want—only we won't want what we get.

By itself, valuing freedom understood in terms of autonomy is karmically problematic. But when combined with a high valuation of equality—as is the case in most liberal, democratic societies and a good many others heading in this direction—the problem is compounded. As core values, autonomy and equality can coexist in a society only if its individual members are effectively able to ignore one another's choices. Otherwise, when your choices differ from mine, they will make a difference, requiring me to adjust my own actions and choices. Your freedom will limit mine, and mine will limit yours. As long as freedom is understood in terms of being able to control our experiential circumstances, equality cannot be achieved unless every-one thinks and chooses exactly alike or unless the consequences of our individual choices are effectively isolated. Either way, we are prac-tically driven toward a satisfied lapse into dramatic entropy—a world in which our differences no longer make any difference and in which choosing is ultimately meaningless. If dramatic entropy should ever reach its maximum—perhaps through nearly complete immersion in virtual realities—we will have nothing at all to offer one another. Although we would at any given instant be able to experience what-ever we might want, we would always be left wanting.

Chan practice undercuts the root conditions of our dramatic impoverishment. In the context of an imperial China in which the value of tradition-determined relationships were highly celebrated and often worked against the realization of truly liberating intimacy among all beings—enforcing, for example, strict codes of behavior that perpetuated gender and class biases—this meant building the resources for conducting ourselves as "true persons without rank." In the context of America and the contemporary world more broadly, where individual autonomy and freedom from all forms of tradition are widely celebrated, countering our dramatic impoverishment through the practice of Chan could well mean clarifying our rela-tionships with others and deepening the lived meaning of ongoing community.

Whatever our context, Chan helps rebuild our capacity for going appropriately "crosswise"—for going against the grain of our own habits and inherited customs to make a real difference, both for our-selves and for others. This is possible only if we are able to read the karma or dramatic complexion of our situation skillfully and respond as needed. To the extent that our emotions consist of dramatic nego-tiations that intensify or alter the meaning of our situation, practicing Chan can be seen as developing emotional maturity and dramatic clarity. It means having the confidence needed to let go of both the arrogance of independence from others and the humiliation of depen-dence on them. Especially under the guidance of a skilled master, practicing Chan is the process of improvising shared and liberating revisions in the meaning of our situation as it has come to be.

For all this, Chan is not a cure-all. The practice of Chan spirituality does not culminate in a once-and-for-all, one-size-fits-all form of salvation. It does not result in an eternal state of freedom. Instead, it is the process of developing, in the midst of our present relationships, the resources needed to travel the infinite path of the bodhisattva. This path is all "middle" with no ends. As pointed out to Mazu, it cannot be seen but only seen from—an actively blazed path of continually demonstrating the meaning of appreciative and contributory genius. Traveling it consists—moment by moment, with wisdom, attentive virtuosity and moral clarity—in bringing out the profound value of our situation, working with and through any and every form of want or suffering toward the shared realization of relating freely. Chan is not a path traveled because of what we will find or be when it is over but because there is simply no better way of traveling.

Does Chan spirituality, then, exclude or overcome other forms of spirituality? If it is precisely Buddhist practice or conduct that is Buddha, must one be Buddhist to be awakened? Chan's own answer—so forcefully stated in Linji's dismissal of concepts like "Buddha" and "Dharma" as "hitching posts for donkeys"—is to cut off the root of such questions. They are only clever tactics for reserving one's individual right to not demonstrate, here and now, the readiness to awaken.

From the Chan perspective, there is ultimately no such thing as Buddhism. There is also no Judaism, Christianity, Islam, or Hinduism. These are all just names and forms created out of our own limited conceptual resources and desires. Finally, like all things, including our own selves, they are empty. Given that, there can be no hard boundaries between them and nothing to obstruct their creative interpenetration. Our one true nature is before name and form, before true and false, before the one and the many. It is before religion and politics and society, and yet it is not in any way ancient or timelessly distant. Our true nature is—simply and gracefully, without any hesitation—doing what cannot be done through benefiting what cannot be benefited.

Further Reading

Contemporary readers embarking on the study of Chan—not unlike the Chinese who, fifteen hundred years ago, were faced with deciding which handful among thousands of Buddhist texts should be considered "essential reading"—are now confronted with a bewilderingly extensive body of literature. Fifty years ago, the number of English-language books related to Chan Buddhism could likely have been counted on the fingers of both hands. If books on Zen were included, that figure might have risen into the range of two to three dozen. Today, any major bookstore will have at least that many Chan and Zen related titles in stock and will be able to order thousands of others. This explosion of books in print has taken place in both trade and academic presses and at all levels of sophistication, with dozens of new titles being added each year.

Here I want to provide some initial guidance in approaching the wealth of materials now available on Chan. For the purpose of addressing the needs of different readers, these suggestions for further reading will be separated into five groups: several books helpful in setting up an overall historical context for the study of Chan; references for the primary sources —in Chinese—from which the quotations from Chan masters in the present volume were drawn; full English translations of these works as well as a small number of other similar primary texts in translation; a modest list of scholarly books that either were useful in writing the present volume or would afford the interested reader a responsible introduction to the vast (and still growing) academic literature on Chan; and, finally, a very small set of references to books by contemporary Chan and Zen masters.

HISTORICAL BACKGROUND

For a very brief, but still comprehensive overview of Buddhism, there is much to recommend the introduction, written by Donald S. Lopez, Jr., to the edited volume *Buddhism in Practice* (Princeton: Princeton University Press, 1995). For a relatively short, readable, and careful treatment of the full range of Buddhist religion, consider *The Buddhist Religion: A Histor-*

ical Introduction (edited by Richard H. Robinson and Willard L. John-son; Belmont, Calif.: Wadsworth Publishing, 1997).

For a more detailed introduction to early Buddhist thought, the classic book by Walpola Rahula *What the Buddha Taught* (New York: Grove Press, 1974) is still among the most accessible. For an introduction to the Mahayana tradition as a whole, with short chapters on both Chinese Buddhism and Chan, I would recommend Paul Williams' *Mahayana Buddhism: The Doctrinal Foundations* (New York: Routledge, 1989).

Perhaps the most accessible and reliable overall history of Chan is found in Heinrich Dumoulin's *Zen Buddhism: A History* (New York: Macmillan, 1994). The first volume of this two-part series focuses on India and China and has very useful introductions to the main figures of the traditional lineages of Chan. It can be usefully supplemented with Kenneth Ch'en, *The Chinese Transformation of Buddhism* (Princeton: Princeton University Press, 1973) and Erik Zurcher, *The Buddhist Conquest of China: The Spread and Adaptation of Buddhism in Early Medieval China* (Leiden: Brill, 1972). Although the last two do not deal exclusively with Chan, they provide usefully detailed and yet comprehensive pictures of Buddhist developments in China.

PRIMARY SOURCES

The selected translations of Chan works appearing in this volume are all my own and were drawn from a variety of sources. Quotes of Bodhidharma and his school are modified from Jeffrey Broughton's English translations of the Chinese texts contained in the *Long Scroll of the Treatise on the Two Entrances and Four Practices* as edited by Yanagida Seizan in his *Daruma no goroku* (Tokyo: Chikuma Shobo, 1969). The selections from Huineng's teachings are from the critical Chinese edition compiled by Philip Yampolsky from the Dunhuang manuscript in the Stein Collection (S5475). Excerpts from the teachings of Mazu were translated from *Jiangxi Mazu daoyi Chanshi yulu* in the *Dazang jing,* volume 45. Selections from Huangbo's teachings were translated from *Huangbo shan duanji Chanshi xin fayao,* as edited in the *Taisho shinshu daizokyo* (Tokyo: Taisho Issaikyo Kankokai, 1924–1933, no. 2012a). The teachings of Linji were also taken from a Taisho edition (T: 1985) of *Zhenzhou Linji huizhao Chanshi yulu.*

PRIMARY SOURCES IN TRANSLATION

All of the primary sources from which passages were selected for this volume have been rendered in complete English translations. The Bodhidharma texts have been translated with commentary by Jeffrey L. Broughton in *The Bodhidharma Anthology: The Earliest Records of Zen* (Berkeley: University of California Press, 1999). While much of the supplemental material in this volume is intended for the specialist scholar, the translation of these earliest Chan documents is both lucid and illuminating and can easily be read on its own.

Likewise, Philip Yampolsky's *The Platform Sutra of the Sixth Patriarch* (New York: Columbia University Press, 1978) includes a translation of the text attributed to Huineng, a scholarly introduction, and a critical Chinese edition of the original Dunhuang text.

The teachings of Mazu have been translated by Cheng Chien Bhikshu as *Sun-face Buddha: The Teachings of Ma-tsu and the Hung-chou School of Chan* (Berkeley: Asian Humanities Press, 1992). Included is a short introduction to the life of Mazu and the school of Chan into which he was initiated.

Huangbo's treatise on the transmission of mind is available as *The Zen Teaching of Huang Po* (New York: Grove Press, 1958). Although rather dated, John Blofeld's translation is generally quite good. Also included in this book is "The Wan Ling Record," a supplemental collection of anecdotes and teachings attributed to Huangbo.

Finally, the teachings of Linji have recently been translated by Burton Watson as *The Teachings of Lin-chi* (New York: Columbia University Press, 1999). An older translation by Irmgard Schlogel, *The Zen Teaching of Rinzai* (Denver: Shambhala Press, 1976), is also a faithful rendering of the lively and vernacular Chinese used in the original.

In addition to these translations of the Chan teachings included in the present volume, several other books of Chan teachings in translation deserve mention. John Blofeld has translated the work of one of Mazu's students, Huihai, in *The Zen Teaching of Instantaneous Awakening by Hui Hai* (Leicester, England: The Buddhist Publishing Group, 1994). This volume makes a nice companion to his Huangbo translation. Also available in translation by Thomas Cleary are *The Sayings and Doings of Pai-chang* (Los Angeles: Center Publications, 1979). A student of Mazu and his direct dharma heir, Baizhang is traditionally known as the author of the Chan monastic code.

Peter N. Gregory has done a very useful translation and introduction to one of the more accessible works by Zongmi, a lineage holder in both the Chan and Huayan traditions, *Zongmi: Inquiry into the Origin of Humanity: An Annotated Translation of Tsung-mi's Yuan jen lun with a Modern Commentary* (Honolulu: University of Hawai'i Press, 1995). This book provides very useful insights into how one of the most academically adept masters of Chinese Buddhism advocated its "completion" of China's indigenous Confucian and Daoist traditions through the concepts of buddha-nature and karma.

SECONDARY SCHOLARSHIP ON CHAN

The scholarly study of Chan has in recent decades generated a great number of works geared to the needs of academic specialists in religious studies, history, anthropology, and philosophy. For the most part, these works approach Chan with a degree of detail that will bewilder the beginning student and be of only tangential use in exploring Chan spirituality. Here I will restrict mention to works and authors that I found useful in preparing the present volume and that I believe will be of benefit to the more academically oriented reader.

Two books by Bernard Faure can be recommended as sophisticated entry points to the scholarship on Chan and Zen: *Ch'an Insights and Oversights: An Epistemological Critique of the Ch'an Tradition* (Princeton: Princeton University Press, 1993) and *The Rhetoric of Immediacy: A Cultural Critique of Chan/Zen Buddhism* (Princeton: Princeton University Press, 1991). Both are excellent examples of the detailed and yet wide-ranging historical and textual analyses being undertaken in contemporary Chan studies aimed at "setting straight" the traditional Chan genealogy.

John McRae's *The Northern School and the Formation of Early Ch'an Buddhism* (Honolulu: University of Hawai'i Press, 1986) is an excellent summary of the best Japanese scholarship on Chan and an insightful rereading of the early tradition that downplays the traditional dialectic between the "sudden" and "gradual" schools of Chan.

For more on this particular theme and the early development of Chan, Peter Gregory's edited volume *Sudden and Gradual Approaches to Enlightenment in Chinese Thought* (Honolulu: University of Hawai'i Press, 1987) and *Early Ch'an in China and Tibet* (edited by Whalen Lai and Lewis Lancaster; Berkeley: University of California Press, 1983) are both good collections, including papers by many of the key researchers on Chan in English.

Among the legacies of Chan are its generation of new forms of literary expression. *The Koan: Texts and Contexts in Zen Buddhism* (edited by Steven Heine and Dale S. Wright; New York: Oxford University Press, 2000) is a very good survey of the current state of the art on this topic. Although this is not a book intended to give insight into the "public case" literature in terms of its use in Chan/Zen training, it does provide useful guidance in thinking through the innovation it represents in the teaching of Chan. For an "insider" view of the literature, *The Gateless Barrier: The Wu-men Kuan (Mumonkan)* (San Francisco: North Point Press, 1990) by Aitken Roshi is both responsible and revealing.

Finally, my own *Liberating Intimacy: Enlightenment and Social Virtuosity in Ch'an Buddhism* (Albany: SUNY, 1995) provides a fuller treatment of the distinctive philosophical dimensions of Chan as understood through its unique forms of Buddhist practice. Of particular interest to some readers would be extended treatments of the meaning of practice in the Chan tradition and of the linkage of Daoist thought, energy work, and the understanding of Chan awakening as relational in nature.

CONTEMPORARY CHAN/ZEN WORKS

Given the emphasis on timely response in Chan and its continued vitality as a lineage of Buddhist practice, it would be remiss not to mention a small number of the Chan or Zen masters whose teachings are available in English. In the late 1950s and early 1960s, when Chan and Zen were beginning to attract a great deal of attention in the United States and Europe, no such works were available. The books of D. T. Suzuki on Japanese Zen were extremely influential but came under considerable critical fire with the boom of new scholarship on Chan and Zen in the 1980s and with growing consideration of the fact that he was not himself a Zen master. Also in the 1960s and early 1970s, many readers were introduced to Chan and Zen through the writings and radio broadcasts of Alan Watts, who was profoundly sympathetic to Buddhist practice but, again, not a lineage holder in any Chan or Zen tradition.

The first book that effectively introduced English reading audiences to the teachings of a contemporary Japanese Zen teacher was *Zen Mind, Beginner's Mind* (New York: Weatherhill, 1970). This collection of marvelously lucid talks given by Soto Zen master Shunryu Suzuki is truly a classic. Published three years earlier was a book by one of the first Americans to be given transmission in a Japanese Zen lineage, Philip Kapleau Roshi. His *The Three Pillars of Zen* (Boston: Beacon Press, 1967) is also a very good introduction to Zen practice. From the Korean tradition of Chan (known as Son), *Only Don't Know* (Cumberland, Rhode Island: Primary Point Press, 1978) is a clear and powerful collection of the teachings and letters to American students of Son master Seung Sahn. *Being Peace* (Berkeley: Parallax Press, 1987) and *The Miracle of Mindfulness: A Meditation Manual* (Boston: Beacon Press, 1996) are good examples of the work by Vietnamese Zen master Thich Nhat Hanh. Although contemporary works in English by masters in Chinese Chan traditions are (for historical reasons) must less prevalent than those by masters in other East Asian traditions, works by Chan master Sheng-yen are widely available, such as *Subtle Wisdom: Understanding Suffering, Cultivating Compassion through Ch'an Buddhism* (New York: Doubleday, 1999).

By no means are these the only contemporary teachers of Chan and Zen whose teachings are available in English. And by no means is it the case that written teachings are published and available for all or even most of the Buddhist teachers now transmitting the legacy of Chan. Many—like my own teacher, Ji Kwang Dae Poep Sa Nim—only engage students directly or through privately circulated writings. Books like those cited above do represent, however, a useful range of starting points for exploring the living response of Chan and Zen to present circumstances and concerns. Ultimately, it is in such responses that the spirit of Chan is most readily and lastingly apparent.

Index

Dimensions of Asian Spirituality

Shinto: The Way Home
Thomas P. Kasulis

Chan Buddhism
Peter D. Hershock

About the Author

Peter D. Hershock is coordinator of the Asian Studies Development Program at the East-West Center. A practicing Buddhist as well as a scholar, his research focuses on applying Buddhist conceptual resources across a broad spectrum of contemporary issues, including technological change and development, human rights, social activism, and the interplay of reason and emotion. Among his publications are *Liberating Intimacy: Enlightenment and Social Virtuosity in Ch'an Buddhism,* a study of the social nature of Ch'an Buddhist liberation, and *Reinventing the Wheel: A Buddhist Response to the Information Age,* a Buddhist critique of the impact of mass mediation and information technology on community and cultural diversity.

Chan Buddhism

Cover and interior designed by Richard Hendel

in Minion, with display type in Tarzana

Composition by Josie Herr

Printing and binding by

The Maple-Vail Book Manufacturing Group

Printed on 60# Text White Opaque, 426 ppi